"Any teacher who wishes to improve their practice for th
benefit from following the clear examples presented in tl
of experience and wisdom gleaned from their own enqu.
by-step guide to conducting educational action research. It is a much-needed addition to the
field of teacher development."

Prof. Lesley Wood, *Director, COMBER, Faculty of Education,*
North-West University, South Africa

"*Action Research for the Classroom*, a 'how to' book on values-based educational action
research in the classroom, is fabulous! The supportive tone, research skills presented in
manageable chunks and practical frameworks, checklists and examples of teacher research
has a 'I can do it!' feel to it. The authors attained their goal of sharing teachers' authentic voices
and inspired me to think deeply about my contributions to a more just and equitable world."

Dr Jacqueline Delong, *International Mentor, Canada*

"This is an essential guide for educators who wish to engage in practitioner based research
in their education settings. Each chapter provides clear guidance on how to embark on and
use Action Research in an education context. Rich insights from practicing educators across
a range of relevant sectors offer valuable advice from their own research journey. I would
encourage educators who are interested in engaging in practice informed research to
examine this text."

Dr Bernadette Wrynn, *Assistant Professor, Coordinator MEd Programme*
(Research in Practice), Froebel Department of Primary and
Early Childhood Education, Maynooth University,
Co. Kildare, Ireland

ACTION RESEARCH FOR THE CLASSROOM

What is action research? Why does it matter in education? This practical and accessible book provides answers to these questions, guiding readers through a meaningful and manageable approach to research in practice. Readers will benefit from guidance on easing the stress of research projects in teacher education courses, professional development initiatives and in school self-evaluation.

Supported by case studies from teachers' and student teachers' practice, chapters guide readers through key aspects of carrying out a research project, including:

- planning a research project
- collecting and using data
- presenting evidence
- generating theory
- writing up and disseminating your research
- a theoretical rationale to show why the research is conducted in this way

Written in an accessible manner by experienced classroom teachers and academic researchers, this book is an essential read for those conducting research on their own practice as part of their professional learning. *Action Research for the Classroom* shows how teacher research is drawn from the reality of busy life in the classroom and that it can be undertaken in the most complex learning environments, creating positive change for teaching and learning.

Máirín Glenn, formerly an experienced school teacher and principal, currently works as an education consultant and a co-convenor of Network for Educational Action Research in Ireland (NEARI). Máirín is passionate about educational action research and its transformational power to enhance practice and promote social justice.

Bernie Sullivan is a committed and passionate action researcher with many years of experience as a teacher and as a school principal. Currently, she lectures on a Masters' program in research in practice and is a tutor on a postgraduate school leadership course. She has co-authored several books on action research and is a co-convenor of NEARI.

Mary Roche, formerly a classroom teacher and experienced lecturer in teacher education at both primary and secondary levels, is currently an education consultant and a school adviser. She is a co-convenor of NEARI, author of *Developing Children's Critical Thinking through Picturebooks* (Routledge, 2015) and co-author of several books on action research.

Caitriona McDonagh is a lecturer of Research in Practice and Research Methodologies. In addition to her writing and research into primary education, she is a co-convenor of NEARI. She holds extensive experience of implementing research in practice as a primary and special education teacher, researcher and teacher educator.

ACTION RESEARCH FOR THE CLASSROOM

A Guide to Values-Based Research in Practice

Máirín Glenn, Bernie Sullivan, Mary Roche and Caitriona McDonagh

Routledge
Taylor & Francis Group

LONDON AND NEW YORK

Designed cover image: © Getty Images

First published 2023
by Routledge
4 Park Square, Milton Park, Abingdon, Oxon OX14 4RN

and by Routledge
605 Third Avenue, New York, NY 10158

Routledge is an imprint of the Taylor & Francis Group, an informa business

British Library Cataloguing-in-Publication Data
A catalogue record for this book is available from the British Library

Library of Congress Cataloging-in-Publication Data
Names: Glenn, Máirín, author. | Sullivan, Bernie, author. | McDonagh, Caitriona, author. | Roche, Mary (Lecturer in education), author.
Title: Action research for the classroom : a guide to values-based research in practice / Máirín Glenn, Bernie Sullivan, Caitriona McDonagh, Mary Roche.
Description: First Edition. | New York : Routledge, 2023. | Includes bibliographical references and index.
Identifiers: LCCN 2022050996 (print) | LCCN 2022050997 (ebook) | ISBN 9781032264134 (Paperback) | ISBN 9781032264127 (Hardback) | ISBN 9781003288183 (eBook)
Subjects: LCSH: Action research in education.
Classification: LCC LB1028.24 .G54 2023 (print) | LCC LB1028.24 (ebook) | DDC 370.72--dc23/eng/20230104
LC record available at https://lccn.loc.gov/2022050996
LC ebook record available at https://lccn.loc.gov/2022050997

ISBN: 978-1-032-26412-7 (hbk)
ISBN: 978-1-032-26413-4 (pbk)
ISBN: 978-1-003-28818-3 (ebk)

DOI: 10.4324/9781003288183

Typeset in Interstate
by MPS Limited, Dehradun

MIX
Paper | Supporting responsible forestry
FSC™ C013985
www.fsc.org

Printed in the United Kingdom
by Henry Ling Limited

CONTENTS

FOREWORD[1]

Stephen Kemmis[2]

This is a terrific book. It aims to help you, the reader, to imagine, prepare for, conduct and report on an educational action research project. It takes you through logical steps to provide relevant help at appropriate times in the process. I'm sure most readers will not just read the chapters in the order they're presented here, but skip back and forth between chapters, dipping into the ideas here and ducking back to follow up on ideas there.

The book puts you at its centre. The authors, Máirín Glenn, Bernie Sullivan, Caitriona McDonagh and Mary Roche, see you as an agentic professional who is, to a greater or lesser extent, realising your educational values through your work as an educator. They invite you to clarify your values not just as a process of personal introspection, but through an unfolding process of reflective engagement with your work and your world - our world, the world. Máirín, Bernie, Caitriona and Mary offer to accompany you on your journey, sharing advice and observations drawn from their long involvement as participants in and observers of educational action research projects. But they are acutely aware that the journey you're about to embark on is your journey, that you'll undertake in your way, engaging with and developing your ideas and values, and preparing for and telling your story.

Many years ago, the famous British action research advocate Lawrence Stenhouse said (1979, p. 7):

> I see academia as a social system for the collaborative production of knowledge through research. Research is a systematic enquiry made public. It is made public for criticism and utilization within a particular research tradition ...

Your action research may open and map new territory, but you travel alongside many thousands of others who have made similar journeys before you and will, I hope, make similar journeys alongside you. Máirín, Bernie, Caitriona and Mary are already at your side. But your journey will be unique. It will take form in your embodied mind and memory, in your engagement with the world, in your reflective journal, and in many texts, documents, records, perhaps including audio and video recordings and transcripts ... Together, this evidence will make sense to you, and perhaps to others, in the story you will tell about what the journey was like, what happened, what the consequences were and where it came to its end - which may of course be a new beginning. Along the way, you will have become part of what Stenhouse called "a social system for the collaborative production of knowledge." You will be doing "systematic enquiry" which you can - I hope you will - "make public." And, if you make your story public, it will be available to others for "criticism and utilization within a particular research tradition" - the vibrant, diverse and evolving tradition of educational action research. And traditions in geography teaching, mathematics, education, educational leadership, nursing, occupational therapy and in many other fields. On a more intimate scale, in conversations, presentations and reports, your "systematic enquiry made public" will also be available for more immediate criticism and utilisation by your friends, critical friends, colleagues, and professional and local communities.

At the moment you may feel you are a newcomer to the field, while others around you (along with Máirín, Bernie, Caitriona and Mary) are "old hands," but you are already on your way through the phase that Lave and Wenger (1991) called "legitimate peripheral participation" (legitimately observing from the sidelines while also "having a go"); you are beginning to develop the "situated knowledge" of the "old hand" - the practically experienced educational action researcher.

I started my journey in educational action research in the mid-1970s, conscious of many who had gone before (like Kurt Lewin in Germany and the US; Stephen Corey in the US; Robert Rapoport in the UK), and, as the 1970s rolled into the 1980s, found myself among such luminaries in educational action research as Lawrence Stenhouse, John Elliott, Clem Adelman and Jack Whitehead in the UK, Paulo Freire (Brazil), Orlando Fals Borda (Colombia), Budd Hall (Canada) and my colleagues Wilfred Carr (then at the University College of North Wales, later at the University of Sheffield), Robin McTaggart, Colin Henry, John Henry at Deakin University in the 1980s. In those days, educational action researchers were fighting for air in the research "paradigm wars" in social and educational science in the 1970s-1980s (Carr and Kemmis 1986). By now, however, action research has secured and established its place in the social and educational research pantheon and it has multiplied and diversified across the globe. Now, you are becoming part of that tradition.

The point of action research is to change the world - your world, our world. To change it for the better. And you will measure your path to making this better world in your own footsteps (Horton and Freire 1990) as you change your own and others' understandings and practices, and the conditions under which we and they practise. To have this self- and world-changing aim is to be committed to praxis - acting for the good of individuals and the good for humankind and life on the planet (Mahon *et al.* 2020). It is to adopt what Anna Stetsenko (2019) called a transformative worldview. It is what you do - what we all do - all the time: "history-making action," making your history, the history of your school or organisation, the history of your community, and writ large, world history. It is to give expression to the kind of curiosity John Dewey (1910) identified: the curiosity that impels our own and others' lives and human development, and the collective development of the societies in which we live.

The road ahead will not all be strewn with rose petals. There will be difficulties, some intellectual, as you struggle with perplexities, and some social, when you come into conflict with established ways of thinking or doing things - "the way we do things around here." You may come face to face with deep-rooted and uncomfortable contradictions about the possibilities for education in an era of schooling. From time to time, you might think the person whose ideas and values are causing you the most trouble is the person whose face you see in the mirror. And that is what action research is for: individual and collective self-reflection. It is a practical way to find paths ahead that lead around and beyond the current untoward consequences of our individual and collective actions, when we discover that the ways we do things now have led or are leading us into unreasonableness, unproductiveness, unsustainability, injustice and undemocratic ways of living.

I once described action research as "a practice-changing practice" (2009). It is a practice directed towards helping people to change their educational (and other) practices. Action research is also an educational practice – it is a form of education for individuals and groups who work and think together about how to change the world for the better. Kemmis *et al.* (Kemmis 2014, p. 26) defined education as:

> ... the process by which children, young people and adults are initiated into particular (1) forms of understanding that aim to foster individual and collective self-expression, (2) modes of action that aim to foster individual and collective self-development, and (3) ways of relating to others and the world that aim to foster individual and collective self-determination.

These individual and collective aims mean that education is always oriented, on the one hand, towards the good for each person and, on the other, towards the good for humankind.

Later, Kemmis and Edwards-Groves (2018, p. 134) added:

> Practices of education aim to initiate students into [1] practices of self-expression, to secure a culture based on reason; ... [2] practices of self-development, to secure a productive and sustainable economy and environment; and ... [3] practices of self-determination, to secure a just and democratic society.

When people do educational action research, they are engaged in a form of self- and collective education of precisely this kind. They aim to foster self-expression, self-development and self-determination for themselves as persons and, collectively, for their profession and their community. And they aim to become better able to participate in a world which secures and sustains cultures based on reason, productive and sustainable economies and environments, and just and democratic forms of social life – in their own lives and work, and in the collective life and work of their profession and their communities. Educational action research is not just research in education, it is research for education: the education of those who undertake it, and for the sake of education in the communities and society in which they undertake it.

As you embark on your educational action research journey, I encourage you to notice that it is a beautiful thing – it is an expression of humanity, solidarity and hope for a better future. It is also an expression of your commitment not just to professionalism, but to your (and our collective) education profession. Most importantly, however, it expresses a deep commitment to your own (and our) education for the generations rising around us, for our human communities and for the community of life on Earth.

Travel well!

Notes

1 Prepared for the volume Glenn, M., Sullivan, B., McDonagh, C. and Roche, M. (in preparation). Action Research for the Classroom. London: Routledge.
2 Stephen Kemmis is Professor Emeritus of Charles Sturt University, New South Wales, and of Federation University, Victoria, Australia. ORCID ID: 0000-0003-2252-8511. Email: stephen@stephenkemmis.com

References

Carr, W. and Kemmis, S. (1986) *Becoming Critical: Knowledge, Education, and Action Research*, London: Falmer.

Dewey, J. (1910) *How We Think*, Lexington, Mass: D.C. Heath.

Horton, M. and Freire, P. (1990) *We Make the Road by Walking: Conversations on Education and Social Change*, Philadelphia, PA: Temple University Press.

Kemmis, S. (2009) 'Action research as a practice-based practice', *Educational Action Research*, 17(3), 463–474.

Kemmis, S. and Edwards-Groves, C. (2018) *Understanding Education: History, Politics, Practice*, Singapore: Springer.

Kemmis, S., Wilkinson, J., Edwards-Groves, C., Hardy, I., Grootenboer, P. and Bristol, L. (2014) *Changing Practices, Changing Education*, Singapore: Springer.

Lave, J. and Wenger, E. (1991) *Situated Learning: Legitimate Peripheral Participation*, Cambridge: Cambridge University Press.

Mahon, K., Heikkinen, L.H.T., Huttunen, R., Boyle, T. and Sjølie, E. (2020) 'What is educational praxis?' in Mahon, K., Edwards-Groves, C., Francisco, S., Kaukko, M., Kemmis, S. and Petrie, K., eds., *Pedagogy, Education, and Praxis in Critical Times*, Singapore: Springer, 15–38.

Stenhouse, L. (1979) 'The problem of standards in illuminative research', *Scottish Educational Review*, 11(1), 5–10.

Stetsenko, A. (2019) 'Radical-transformative agency: Continuities and contrasts with relational agency and implications for education', *Frontiers in Education*, 4(148), available doi: 10.3389/feduc.2019.00148.

ACKNOWLEDGEMENTS

Action research is never done alone. Neither are books about action research. We stand on the shoulders of giants and we recognise the invaluable contribution to our knowledge of people like Maxine Greene, Nel Noddings, Paulo Freire, Jack Whitehead, Jean McNiff, Stephen Brookfield and the many others who have had an educative influence in our learning.

We particularly wish to acknowledge **Professor Stephen Kemmis,** who has been so supportive of our work and who has generously provided the foreword to this publication.

We are indebted also to the following educators who have allowed us to share their ideas and extracts from their research. We authors admire the sincerity, integrity and rigour of their critically reflective work. A heartfelt *'Go Raibh Maith Agat'* to each.

Aisling Connaughton
John Cullinane
Cassandra O'Donnell
Helen O'Farrell
Greg Joynt
Aideen Kenny
Joy Mounter
Ruth Sheridan
Maggie, Norma and Paul who shared their work anonymously.

We are very grateful also to **The Network of Educational Action Research in Ireland** - our many colleagues and friends in the NEARI community - with whom, and from whom, we have learned so much over the past eight years. We are delighted to share some of what we have learned from them in this book.

Thanks too, to the **Routledge** team who have, as usual, been professional and cooperative.

Introduction

You have committed to doing a research project in your classroom and you are excited about that. You have begun in a positive way by buying or borrowing this book, and we, Máirín, Bernie, Caitriona and Mary, hope now to guide you through some new vocabulary and new ideas, as we help you to do action research in ways that support what you value most about your work in the classroom.

We authors have conducted our own classroom research and want to share with you what we have learned from our experiences in teaching, teacher-education and research over the past 30 years. Along with our experience of researching our own classroom practices, we have also worked in several trans-generational and trans-institutional settings, supporting education students and teachers at all levels as they conducted action research in their classrooms. Many teachers feel swamped and demotivated currently (Moeller *et al.* 2018); some, by what seems like poor, conflicting and ever-changing educational policies. We are convinced of the importance of you being in control of your own professional development and researching what is important to you.

The form of action research that we will now guide you through can not only help you to enhance your practice, it can also support teacher resilience and autonomy, contribute to strong educational leadership and generally move towards a more just and equitable world. This is a form of research that is suitable for any context in your work – school leader, classroom teacher, head teacher, special needs teacher, lecturer in teacher education, among others. It is also suitable for any specialism in your work that you might like to investigate – language, technology, leadership, music, guidance, well-being and so on.

An invitation to the reader

The purpose of this book is to enable teachers and student teachers – in particular those who are new to action research in the classroom – to undertake a research project and to produce a report on it. Throughout the book, you will hear the voices of other practitioner researchers as they speak about their experiences.

You who are new to the educational action research process will be encouraged to enhance or improve your practice, to celebrate it or to gain a deeper understanding of it, while

DOI: 10.4324/9781003288183-1

developing a more acute awareness of the importance of your role as educators and of the potential of your influence to make the world a better place. We invite you, then, to join us in exploring ideas, reflecting on your actions and creating new knowledge – all for the betterment of your professional lives and, potentially, for the lives of others in your work setting.

As you read through the book, you will find detailed guidelines on how to carry out a research project in your practice. There are exercises for you to engage with at each step of the educational action research process. We suggest that you try to complete these tasks as comprehensively as possible, so that you will benefit from your reading of the book and gain a competent knowledge of how to undertake the process. Armed with the skills and knowledge required to carry out research, we hope that you will feel confident and sufficiently empowered to begin your research journey. The step-by-step approach in the book will enable you to build your knowledge base gradually and at your own pace. It will also afford you the opportunity to return and reread any section that you may not have grasped fully on your first reading of it. We hope that you will return to the book again and again, either to clarify any concepts that resonate with you or to consolidate your understanding of the essential steps in carrying out educational action research in your practice.

Carrying out your research will bring you to the halfway point of your journey: we encourage you to complete the journey by sharing your research story with others. You might choose to do this at a staff meeting or in a wider setting at district level. You might decide to share some slides, do a podcast or blog or write an account of your research project. Committing the narrative of your research to paper will help to focus your mind on the learning you have gained and the new knowledge you have created through engaging in your research. It will provide an opportunity for you to generate and articulate the theory of your practice that may emerge from the process of carrying out your research. A presentation or a written account may act as a stimulus to disseminate your research among others, for example colleagues, who may be influenced to emulate your research endeavours. A written report may also inspire you to present your research findings at an educational conference, or to submit them to an educational research journal, thus expanding the opportunities of exerting an influence in more widespread social formations (Whitehead 2018).

We invite you to engage wholeheartedly with the educational action research approach that we outline in this book. We hope that your experience, as you engage in research in your practice, will be positive and that it enhances your learning, your understanding and your commitment to improving your practice continuously. Bear in mind that your research project should not be a solitary undertaking but instead, should be carried out with the support and cooperation of others. To this end, the format that we use throughout is one in which we see ourselves as accompanying you on your research journey, providing guidance, assistance and encouragement in an easily accessible manner.

The book, the authors and why researching your practice is important for you

The book

This is a book for those doing research as part of teacher education courses, at degree and postgraduate level, for practising teachers undertaking professional development, and for school leaders supporting research in schools.

We advocate an *educational action research* approach that is values-based; focuses on the centrality of the "self" of the practitioner and their voice; aims towards the enhancement of practice; works towards a fairer and more equitable world and generates theory that has immediate relevance for your classroom, and, possibly for the wider educational milieu.

The main features of the book are as follows:

- the book outlines a step-by-step framework for doing an educational action research project on one's practice – from preparation, to starting to share the completed project with others, as well as generating a living-theory from that process
- educational action research is based on the real life and practice of the teacher or student teacher. It can therefore be undertaken at any time in the life of a school as it embraces all the difficulties that arise in schools, including when interrupted by a global pandemic
- each of the chapters is presented in three sections, with practical advice, relevant real-life research examples from teacher researchers and a theoretical rationale to show why the research is conducted in this way
- it also clarifies common misconceptions about educational research and practical challenges that can arise. These include difficulties that may arise both for student teachers and practising teachers such as lack of time, difficulties with ethical data collection, academic pressures, as well as difficulties with Covid-19

The authors

We authors, Máirín, Bernie, Caitriona and Mary would like now to introduce ourselves and our research. As mature teachers we began our individual research journeys by conducting action research in our own classrooms. In addition to completing PhDs, in which we investigated our practices as teachers through educational action research, we have spent the past 30 years in teacher education contexts. Along with our work with student teachers, we also support teachers who range from those beginning their research journeys to experienced teacher educators and researchers across all levels of education. You can find out more about our work on the website we created – Educational Action Research in Ireland (www.eari.ie). The archive and current activities of the Network for Educational Action Research in Ireland (NEARI), which we established, are on that site. Our research journeys and work experiences have convinced us that one of the main problems is that, often, peoples' research aspirations tend to become somewhat diluted in practice, and so we have written this book specifically for you, whether you are a teacher or a student teacher, as you set out to conduct research in your classroom.

Why this book is important for you

You, like many teachers and student teachers, may have a passion for your work in the classroom. Often this stems from a curiosity about how to do more for your pupils. Dewey (1933) suggests that such curiosity is grounded in characteristics such as open-mindedness, responsibility and whole-heartedness, all of which extend us as professionals. This book will support you in becoming that extended professional teacher (Hoyle 1975) through capturing evidence-informed practice and theorising it by:

- introducing you to how you might undertake an educational action research project
- encouraging you to improve your practice and live more closely to your innermost beliefs and values
- giving you a vehicle to have your voice heard
- helping you discover your sense of agency and autonomy
- inviting you to take a critical look at your practice
- encouraging you to challenge your own assumptions about teaching, learning, classroom cultures and the many power dynamics in which education is embedded
- disrupting the encroaching deprofessionalisation of teachers
- making you aware of the "magic" of educational action research
- providing a framework for how you can research your practice
- encouraging you to persist despite any obstacles that might arise

What you will find in this book

This book involves taking time out to think about yourself and your practice, so that you might be encouraged to engage in an educational action research project, with a view to enhancing that practice. It invites you to be a researcher; to find your own sense of identity and bring yourself and your own core values to your teaching and to your research. We authors feel that this framework will also allow you as a practising teacher to focus on the positive, when carrying out your research, so that you might experience a sense of empowerment. This could help you to feel that you are in control of your own professional development and your environment (Sullivan *et al.* 2021). We feel that this book supports teacher well-being and resilience. We have designed it so that it contributes to relational learning and can contribute to educational leadership, all of which are key features of a sustainable professional body.

The seven chapters in this book largely follow the stages of doing an educational action research project. They are specifically designed for those beginning to research their teaching. All chapters are structured similarly and will contain the following sections:

- **Practicalities:** Each chapter begins with a practical exercise element which will help you to think critically and will contribute to the creation of your final project. Working through the "Task checklist" of activities will enable you to complete your action research project, prepare a report on your research and think about disseminating your work.
- **Examples from teachers and student-teachers:** Following this are real-life stories of teacher researchers from a range of countries and from a variety of levels of teaching.
- **Underpinning theory:** You will then be introduced to some theory that supports the tasks and that will explain why such activities are important in educational action research.
- **Additional reading suggestions and resources:** At the end of each chapter, you will find a list of useful readings, some of which are open-access, and resources.

Chapter 1, *Preparation for a Research Project,* is the opportunity to think about yourself and what makes you unique as a teacher. This chapter outlines how to reflect on your practice, develop a new sense of awareness, play with ideas about what you might like to research, reflect on why you chose this and what is important in your professional life, read about issues that are of interest to you, establish a critical friend and share ideas with them. Finally, it will explain what action research is and what is different about educational action research in the classroom.

Chapter 2, *Getting Started*, shows how you can make your research project specifically about anything you want to change in your practice, about something you would like to celebrate or even to understand at a deeper level. There are suggestions on gentle ways to begin your writing process and how you might discuss your reflections with your constructive or critical friend. As you work through activities in this chapter you also learn to place your practice in the broader context of your influence on society and to investigate how you might make the world a better place.

In Chapter 3, *Planning a Research Project,* you will look at your practice and focus on the significance of your values throughout the whole research process. Articulating your values is essential when conducting quality action research in classrooms because values are the underpinning foundations and overarching principles towards which we aspire as teachers. By reflecting on and answering a series of questions you will be assisted in identifying your educational values and in checking to see if these values are being realised in your practice or not.

More practical activities, such as how to begin collecting data and what kinds of data, are in Chapter 4, *Collecting and Using Data*. This will help provide a clear brief description of your practice for others, who can only see into your classroom via your written account. You will learn how to collect data in ways to show that you are giving an honest account of your situation. You will find ways to show changes in your thinking and improvement in your practice as your project progresses. Finally, you will be mining your data for examples of enhanced practice, new insights into practice and links between your values and your practice.

Chapter 5, *Presenting Evidence: Values as Research Standards*, guides you in how you might present evidence of your new learning from your research. Data does not speak for itself and should only be considered to be appropriate when it can be aligned with the values you hold. We show how this can be done here by establishing standards that are drawn from your values. When you have data that meets your research standards, they can be presented as evidence of your claim to new learning. You will find out how other teacher researchers present their new learning to others to establish if their claim is honest and valid.

Chapter 6, *Generating Theory and Its Significance*, will shows you how, as an educational researcher, you generate theory from your practice. This simply means that you offer descriptions and explanations for your new learning (Whitehead and McNiff 2006). Throughout your research, you will not only think about how you might describe your practice and your learning, but also how you might explain what happened, why it happened and what its purpose might be. This process will be explained in detail with case studies. Action researchers explicitly state the significance of their research when they make their research public or by writing up their dissertation or research report.

We provide a structure for writing a research report in Chapter 7, *Writing Up and Disseminating: Sharing the Story of Your Learning*. You can begin the practice-writing process at the very outset of your project by using your reflective journal as a trial writing process. We will guide you in utilising your academic reading to inform your writing. Academic writing involves drafting and redrafting your work. You can begin a draft of a literature review or a methodology chapter early in the course of your research. You will redraft and refine your writing as time goes on, and this will help you when it comes to the formal writing up of your project.

We feel that the following are three key features of the research approach we have recommended.

Our educational action research approach is:

- **educational** in that it is based in a philosophy that is educational, focused on demonstrating its influence in learning and constantly challenging us to ask why things are as they are
- it involves critically evaluating real-life **action** in the classroom, a process which is complex and ever-changing
- it is **research** that requires us to explicitly identify the values by which its quality can be judged and from which theory is generated

You will learn how to research in a philosophical way because, in studying your own practice, and the values that underpin that practice, you are engaging with the fundamental nature of knowledge and reality at an academic level. *Philosophia*, in its original Greek etymology, means love of wisdom. The theory you will develop about your practice will be grounded in your journey to understand what cannot be reduced solely to rigid categories, simple definitions or tick-box standards.

Your research will be axiological, or values-based, throughout. You will identify epistemological values about the meaning of knowledge and how it is created in your practice.

You will also articulate your ontological values – including your personal, professional, ethical values.

Your values base needs to be made explicit throughout your classroom research. You will begin by identifying "value tensions" (Coghlan and Brannick 2005, p. 135) in how you work. Like Leitch (2018, p. 162), your living paradox stimulates "personal anxiety but, ultimately, the capacity to accommodate the tensions" through your research approach. You will investigate your values and eventually explain how they are the standards by which the quality of your research can be judged.

Overall, in this book we offer each reader the option of designing their educational action research process according to their own values.

1 Preparation for a research project: What is educational action research?

This chapter is about dipping your toe into the water as you begin doing values-based research in your practice. It is about putting some preparation in place, seeing how other teachers have engaged with such projects and finding out why research in practice is important.

There are three sections in this chapter, in which:

- we explore some practical tasks that may be of use when preparing for classroom research projects
- we draw on practical examples from teachers who have researched their own practice
- we outline what educational action research in the classroom is, its key features and why it is important.

It is worth noting that throughout this book, we will use the term "educational action research" to refer to the values-based research that can be undertaken in one's practice with the aim of enhancing it and, at the same time, working towards a better, more just and more equitable world as we try to make a difference for good (Roche 2015). As teachers and as researchers we hope to "act educationally in the sense of acting for the good for each person and for the good for humankind" (Kemmis 2012, p. 885). While undertaking educational action research, the researcher generates their own educational theory from their practice.

Section 1: Preparation for a classroom research project

This section suggests some practical steps to take as you begin your classroom research project. We believe that spending time on preparation for your project will help you to engage with the research process more fully and more meaningfully. We will outline the preparation in terms of initial tasks, reflection tasks and writing tasks.

Initial tasks

In these tasks we encourage you to first stop, pause and reflect on your work as a teacher in order to develop a heightened sense of awareness about what happens daily in your classroom. Take time to do some professional reading and to seek out some critical friends.

DOI: 10.4324/9781003288183-2

Stop, pause and reflect on your work as a teacher

Pausing and reflecting is not always easy for educators – at any level of the education system. In 2001, Dadds and Hart spoke about the "hurry-along curriculum" (p. 49) and things have not become any calmer since then. Many teachers will attest to the busyness of the school day (Davison 2015; Deasy and Mannix McNamara 2016). University lecturers and college tutors are finding life just as harried. They are often required to research, to "publish or perish" on top of their work of lecturing, assessing, supervising, leading and designing modules, as well as supporting students (Hodgins and Mannix McNamara 2021; Pepper 2022).

It is clear therefore that all teachers need to take some time to stop, pause and reflect on their work as a teacher. In many cases, that will most likely take place after school. Maxine Greene (1984) says that taking time to think things through is like having an "internalized dialogue … through which we talk things over with ourselves" (p. 55). She argues that we need to stop and think because we proceed in an unthinking manner for much of the time. She suggests that we are:

> … "caught up" in dailyness, in the sequences of tasks and routines. Of course we have to proceed that way a good deal of the time, but there should be moments when we deliberately try to draw meaning out of particular incidents and experiences.
>
> (Greene 1984, p. 55)

Making meaning from our professional lives lies at the heart of educational action research. Greene reminds us that we must stop and reflect as we try to draw meaning out of experiences. She says that such meaning-making requires "a pause, a conscious effort to shake free of what Virginia Woolf called 'the nondescript cotton wool' of daily life" (Greene 1984, p. 55).

Greene's claim (1984) that we need to take the time for reflectiveness about ourselves and our work is as relevant in the challenging times in which we live now as when it was written nearly 40 years ago. In fact, even longer ago, the Greek philosopher Socrates is reputed to have stated that the unexamined life is not worth living (Famakinwa 2012, p. 97).

Developing awareness

Engaging in educational action research implies that you develop a new awareness around your practice and your thinking about it. Try to tune in to life in your classroom as closely as you can in terms of listening more carefully, watching more attentively and sensing more intently. Developing keener antennae is part of the preparation you may undertake in the initial stages of the research process as you develop your sense of personal awareness, intellectual awareness and relational awareness (Glenn 2021a). Make short notes to yourself throughout the day. These will help you to remember and to make sense of your work when you reflect on it at a later stage.

With that in mind, it is probably a good idea to choose a time that is suitable for you to reflect on your work. Deciding to do it once a week on a Friday night might suit some people, but you may be too tired then to give the reflection the energy it needs. We authors suggest that it is best to put time aside every day. Reflection is an action that requires effort and engagement: it is not easy to do and there is no best way that suits all. We recommend, therefore, that you try to establish a daily routine. You need to choose a time and a place where you will have at least 15 uninterrupted minutes, free from the distraction of everyday life, to think about what is important for you in your school work. Think about why these issues are important for you. Think about the values you hold and see if you can make any connections between them and the way you think about your work as well as the way you actually work. Play with the ideas. Educational action research embraces challenges and draws on real life, warts and all. In developing a new awareness around their practice, teachers often become aware of the messy aspect of researching their own practice. It is rarely straightforward and for many, the mess becomes the research (Cook 2009; Mellor 2001).

Articulating your thoughts may take some time. Don't be worried by this. We all know far more than we realise. Greene (1984, p. 60) says that when we are thinking about our practice, "we cannot but recognize how much more we know than we can ever say." Citing Polanyi (1962), Greene suggests that this is testimony to the "tacit awareness that underlies what we have learned … [and] to a sense of personal engagement with what we have come to understand, a consciousness of our human desire to keep knowing more, to extend what Polanyi called 'personal knowledge'" (Greene 1984, p. 60).

Professional reading

To begin your professional reading, we suggest that you might start with that 1984 paper *How do we think about our craft?* by Maxine Greene. It is available online at https://maxinegreene.org/uploads/library/how_we_think_craft.pdf. While this is not a new paper, it contains many insightful ideas that can help you to become aware of how you think about your teaching.

If you are not doing an accredited programme with an institution or university, then access to good academic papers can be difficult. Don't worry – there is also a large repository of freely accessible papers available at the Directory of Open Access Journals at https://doaj.org. Many traditional journals now provide an increasingly good range of open-access papers. See our suggestions for reading and the list of resources at the end of this and every chapter.

Choose one or two papers that you find interesting and then, having read them, ask yourself why they appealed to you, what you have learned or are curious about, and if you agree or disagree with the ideas presented. In the bibliography sections of those papers, you may find other articles that catch your attention. You might find it useful to begin by reading the abstract, which is a summary of the paper, and then reading the conclusion in order to get a quick overview or a sense of the content of the paper. You can decide then if you want to read the whole paper. Research journals each have their specific focus and a peer-reviewed paper means that the journal's team of research experts decide if the paper has met the journal's specific criteria for publication. If you intend to write an academic research report it may be worth noting the layout and language used in peer-reviewed papers.

Invite some people to become critical friends

It is important now that you think deeply about who you might invite to be your critical friend or friends. Critical friends are people who know you, and know and understand your work. They will be chosen for their candour and honesty. You would like them to listen to you, engage critically with your ideas and ask you the difficult questions that make you reflect deeply on what you are saying or doing.

When you invite people to be your critical friends, explain what you want them to do and ask for their permission in writing to use whatever data they provide. You may run ideas past them for feedback; you could ask them to play devil's advocate and say "Yes – but what if?"; you might invite them to sit in on a lesson in your classroom and observe, if possible. You should be able to trust that they will provide constructive and critical feedback that will lead you to deepen your own knowledge and understanding through reflecting on what they say. It is unlikely that just one person can fulfil all of these roles but you can have more than one critical friend. During conversations with them – face to face or via the phone or email – you will listen carefully and enter into a real dialogue with them. As we will see in Chapter 4, you can also record these conversations (with appropriate permission) and submit them to your critical friend for eva-luation. In this way they will form part of your data. Ultimately it will be your own decision to take their advice or not, but through rigorous reflection and reflexivity, you should be able to learn from their dialogue with you. There is a good exploration of what critical friendship involves in Baskerville and Goldblatt (2009). In Chapter 2 we will give an example of this process in action.

Reflection tasks

In the initial tasks above, you have already begun to reflect seriously on your work and what it means to you. You may have also considered what others say through your professional reading and ideas from your critical friends. Now it is time to collect your thoughts together for the purpose of research. Begin to write your reflective journal. You can find more about the process of critical reflection in Sullivan *et al.* (2016).

Writing tasks

Your reflective journal is a storehouse for your thinking and will be a key source of your data. In later chapters we will show how it can develop into a place for analysing your data too. It is a good idea to put away your phone and the distraction of social media for periods of re-flection, thinking and writing. Take out a notebook or jotter and a pen or favourite writing instrument. Write the date on the top of the page and then clear your mind.

As an opening activity, you could try asking yourself – and answering – the following questions:

What makes me happiest when I am teaching. Why?
What do I do really well? Why?
What bothers me about teaching?
What do I find most difficult? Why?

What brought me to teaching?
Why is teaching important to me?

By beginning with any one of these questions, you may find something that makes you stop in your tracks. Highlight it, if this happens, and ask yourself why this is important. Try to determine why it is of interest or concern to you. Unpack it or, if you are tired, earmark it for deeper consideration later. By doing this regularly you may develop a heightened sense of awareness about your work and begin to develop critical thinking skills.

Write a short synopsis of your current favourite educational article and explain why it is important to you. This could also serve as draft writing for a literature review for a report.

To prepare for your research project, see if you can write down what your values are; what might draw you to action research and what the benefits and shortcomings of educational action research might be. This could also be useful as a draft writing for a section on methodology for a report.

We have summarised and compiled these tasks into a list below (Figure 1.1). Please note that this list is merely a suggestion that may be of help. It is not exhaustive and you should modify it to suit your own situation.

Tasks to help prepare for your educational action research project

Initial tasks	Yes	No	Under way
Stop, pause and reflect on your work as a teacher	___	___	___
Develop a heightened sense of awareness	___	___	___
Do some professional reading	___	___	___
Develop some critical friends	___	___	___
Reflection tasks	Yes	No	Under way
What is important for you in your school work? Why?	___	___	___
What values do you hold? What connections can you make between your values and your work?	___	___	___
Can you see contradictions, inconsistencies or 'mess' in your work?	___	___	___
Writing Tasks	Yes	No	Under way
Begin to write a reflective journal	___	___	___
Write a short synopsis of your current favourite educational article and explain why it is important to you. (As draft writing for a literature review for a report)	___	___	___
See if you can write down what your values are.	___	___	___
What might draw you to action research?	___	___	___

Figure 1.1 Tasks to help prepare for an educational research project

Section 2: How some teachers engage with educational action research

For decades, teachers have been undertaking educational action research for their own professional development, for accreditation, for the benefit of their schools and school districts. Many of their accounts are inspirational. Many have undertaken research in their practice during the restrictions and challenges of Covid-19, and their accounts capture the difficulties both teachers and pupils experienced during that time.

Most forms of action research are values-based. This means that the values the researcher holds play an integral role in the research process. We include some examples here to show how teachers engaged with their research in their practice.

Helen O'Farrell undertook her educational action research in her practice as a primary-level teacher in 2018. Her passion was reading and literature, and she hoped to understand how she could enhance children's empathy through the implementation of a fictional literature programme. As Helen examined her values, she realised that she was experiencing herself as a "living contradiction" as outlined by Whitehead (1989; 2018), where she found that on close examination, her values did not correspond with how she taught reading. We will discuss the concept of experiencing oneself as a living contradiction in greater detail in Chapter 2. She claims that she was teaching reading to her class of 11-year-olds "in a stagnant, unimaginative way" (O'Farrell 2018, p. 19). She sought to enhance her teaching of reading as she worked more closely to her values.

She outlines her ontological values, a concept that will be explained in Section 3, here:

> The symbiosis of empathy, care and social justice form the basis of my ontological values system. Emanating from these values is my acute social conscience. For instance, I am passionate about the children showing care and empathy for one another and developing an understanding that no-one is binary – good or bad – instead we are complex, nuanced beings who deserve empathy and understanding. I strive to listen and respond appropriately to all of the children and gain an understanding of where they are "coming from" (Demetriou, 2018, p. 3) and I hope that they will replicate these behaviours. Indeed, I am drawn to Noddings' (1995) idea that the most valuable lesson we can teach children is to care for others and to develop an awareness that they themselves are cared for and understood too.

Helen continues with her reflections and makes a direct link between her values-led research and its potential significance for working towards a better and more just world. She writes:

> Furthermore, in a broader sense, I often find myself despairing at the apathy, lack of empathy and even systematic xenophobia shown to certain groups in society, such as refugees and other minorities, particularly in a world that increasingly views the "other" as a threat to our own, western values. Indeed, this is further heightened by my awareness that the children I teach, live and learn in largely homogeneous environments, have little contact with minority groups. I worry that they may be prone

to believing the often ubiquitous stereotypes presented to them. As a teacher-researcher, I endeavour to disrupt the expansion of racist ideologies so that the children in my care can become agents of positive change for the future and practise greater empathy and acceptance.

Helen describes how she further experienced herself as a living contradiction:

While I explored my values of empathy, care and social justice, I was forced to confront the uncomfortable truth that I was failing in these areas too …

While my desire to live out my values of empathy, care and social justice was alive, it was diminished by the demands of a heavily laden curriculum and a distinct lack of knowledge of how to go about it. I found myself talking to the children about "how lucky" we all are, allowing myself and them to fall victim to jaded platitudes, clichés and "the passive gaze that is the hallmark of our time" (Greene 1995, p. 13). Yet, through my encounters with the works of scholars like Freire (1985), Greene (1980) and Rosenblatt (1978; 1994), I came to learn the power literature has to make meaningful change and move pupils to see things in new ways so that they can ultimately become more "wide-awake" (Greene 1980) and create a more just society.

Helen's personal and professional learning was substantial:

I no longer feel the same pressure to subscribe to the surface types of literacy instruction that used to characterise my teaching. Through the action research process and the power of reflective practice, I have connected with my values and improved my classroom practices (Kemmis, 2009). Additionally, I have a newfound resolve to incorporate themes like awareness of power and critique into my teaching and in doing so begin what Greene (1995) describes as a change in consciousness and a new awareness of possibility, towards a Pedagogy of Democratisation (Giroux, 2011) where children can begin to create change. This drive to foster critical thinking and interrogate what is deemed acceptable in our society is commensurate with my epistemological values too as I believe that knowledge is constructed through experience and dialogue.

Helen's practice as well as her understanding of her practice has now changed:

The pressures of teaching in the primary school classroom dictate that we, as teachers, place a disproportionate emphasis on the more academic subjects, to the detriment of incorporating themes of care and empathy. For a long time, I did not believe that I was assuming the identity of a "good" teacher unless I was teaching the "core" subjects daily. Indeed, from conversations with fellow teachers, this sentiment is ubiquitous. However, the fruits I have borne both personally and professionally, in addition to the gains experienced by the children through my deviation from the norm, have been liberating.

Helen's research account shows how her own tenacity and hope managed to overcome the difficulties she encountered within herself and in her teaching.

Some other classroom researchers experienced nearly insurmountable difficulties in the process of the research. For example, Cassandra O'Donnell's (2021) study was about her journey of developing the vocabulary and expressive language skills of her pupils who were in their first year in an urban primary school. She explored the development of oral language skills through play as she worked towards living more closely to her values of respect, trust, compassion and creativity. The Covid-19 pandemic impacted deeply on her research plan – especially as her teaching and her data collection moved online. She wrote:

As a consequence of the Covid-19 pandemic, teaching and learning moved online throughout the months of January and February 2020. Initially, I had intended that the research, and subsequent data collection, would begin online in January. However, due to the discovery that the enthusiasm levels and responses from the children were much lower than anticipated, data collection proved almost impossible and so, the research was paused temporarily.

While undertaking research in the classroom can be fraught with unforeseen challenges, the insight and support of critical colleagues should never be underestimated. Cassandra shows how she dealt with her concern about her difficulties with collecting data from her very young children during the pandemic. She continues:

During conversations with my supervisor, it came to light that this "lack of data" was in fact, data in itself. It highlighted the cruciality of in-person teaching in relation to the development of children's oral language skills, and the difficulties in engaging sufficiently with younger children, through the online medium.

Even though Cassandra was disappointed because her research did not go exactly as she had planned it, she still gained important insights into her practice as a teacher – precisely *because* it did not go according to plan.

The excerpts above highlight how educational action research is a powerful form of research for the classroom. It can enable the teacher researcher to enhance their practice and to develop new insights into it as they try to enact their values in their everyday work. While the process may be difficult and messy sometimes, it can also instigate a way of being and of teaching that can inspire us towards a better world.

Section 3: What is educational action research and why is it important?

When preparing for your project, it is worth considering what type of research you will use and why you have chosen it. While many accredited courses require a specific research approach, it is important for teachers to be sure that the research they do in their classrooms reflects the complexity of their work and has integrity. So, in this section we explore the importance of educational action research. We clarify why it is a research approach that has enabled many teacher researchers (including Helen and Cassandra) to enhance their practice, to develop new knowledge about it and, importantly, to instigate a way of being and of teaching that may inspire them towards a better world.

We explain all this under the following headings:

- what makes research educational
- key elements of educational action research
- the importance of educational action research

What makes research educational?

Education is about self-improvement, learning more about ourselves, about others and our worlds as we make new meanings together. It requires change. Educational action research includes learning with values of human flourishing according to Whitehead (2018). We believe that it requires enhancing one's practice, learning from that process and generating theory from it. Key features that support such changes are a focus on "I" as a teacher and researcher; on what *I* have learned to value as a person and as a professional within my world; and sustaining this form of research. We will now discuss what each of these means and how they are linked to research that is educational, keeping in mind the broader context of what it means to live an examined life, as Socrates suggests, for the benefit of others.

A focus on "I"

Educational change happens at both the personal and professional levels. For teachers, it can also involve changing familiar and habitual practices. Bassey (1990) says that one of the defining aspects of an action research report, paper, dissertation or thesis is its use of "I". Scientific research often refers to the author or the researcher and speaks in the passive voice – "it was found that ... ." In action research we take ownership of the knowledge, and we refer to ourselves not as a distant "researcher" or "author" but as the immediate "I". This has political implications for educational research – a matter we deal with later in this section.

Coming to terms with the "I" and the ever-emergent sense of identity that it implies, is well outlined by Palmer (2017). He reminds us that teaching cannot be "reduced to technique; good teaching comes from the identity and integrity of the teachers" (p. 12). Becoming a teacher is not just about following technical instructions and meeting the expectations of governing bodies (although that must be done too) – it is also about developing your identity as a teacher, about bringing your whole self, your identity and integrity into the process. It involves coming to know yourself and making a connection with your pupils and colleagues.

Teaching mirrors the soul according to Palmer (2017) and when you begin your educational action research, you bring that sense of self-discovery, of unearthing who you are and the beliefs and values that you hold.

"I" to "we"

While acknowledging that educational action research focuses on the individual doing research in their own practice, there are also possibilities for groups of teachers or whole school teams to come together to research their work collaboratively. Such projects should be based on negotiated, agreed or shared values with a common aim or purpose, where the teacher/researchers would form a collaborative learning community (Glenn *et al.* 2017). Participating staff in schools find such projects to be both worthwhile and energising (Glenn *et al.* 2012) as well as being useful for school self-evaluation.

Values

Educational action research is deeply values-based. We begin by identifying our educational values, and this is where your reflective journal will come into its own. Taking time to reflect on your values, and to record your reflections in your journal, is very important. We have outlined at the beginning of this chapter some of the questions that might help you to begin the process of identifying and then articulating your educational values. When you have identified the things that really matter to you in education, you will then take a long hard look at your practice and ask yourself if these values would be visible to someone observing you at work. Gorman (2021, p. 16) reminds us: "For there is always light. If only we're brave enough to see it. If only we're brave enough to be it." In other words, when we engage in educational action research, we strive to *be* our values in our everyday lives. This is not always an easy task and educational action research often captures the nuances of that struggle. In Roche (2011a), Mary described how she felt a sense of unease and unhappiness about her practice because she valued dialogical pedagogy, yet continued for many years to favour a monological classroom (p. 329). That paper outlines the struggle she engaged in to improve her practice. Throughout all our books (McDonagh *et al.* 2012/2020; Sullivan *et al.* 2016; Glenn *et al.* 2017), we, authors, emphasise unpacking our values and the assumptions we hold about teaching and learning. Throughout this book we will refer to values quite often also, because our research process is informed by them, and they act as guidelines for turning data into evidence – which will be explained further in Chapter 5.

Two interesting terms that can help in understanding values are ontology and epistemology. Your ontological values are an explanation of your personal reality and how you view yourself within your world. Research evidence suggests that decisions to join the teaching profession are very often based on the most noble and altruistic intentions – to contribute to the lives of children and young people, to make a difference through the transformative power of education (see Marsh 2015). These drivers that may motivate the profession are intensely personal and ontological values. They clearly link to an "I" focus. Epistemological values are based on the Greek word *episteme,* which pertains to knowledge. They are about what you mean by knowledge and how you believe that new knowledge is created. These categories of values explain how people learn and how knowledge is transferred between people, and are therefore important in classroom research. These ideas about values will be discussed further in later chapters.

A sustainable educational research approach

We have found (McDonagh *et al.* 2020) that educational action research is not just an intervention, but that it becomes a way of life for teacher researchers. When we authors examined practitioner enquiry and action research, we found that educational action research approaches "combine the personal and the professional aspects of the lives of teachers in a holistic effort to ensure the physical, emotional and mental well-being of the teaching profession" (Sullivan *et al.* 2021, p.15). Throughout this book you will read about the steps you might take as a teacher-researcher to generate theory as you research your practice. Accounts of classroom researchers offer what Zeichner (1999) describes as "a challenge to academic theories of teacher education that are formulated at a distance from the practice of teacher education" (p. 12). We also believe (Glenn *et al.* 2022, np) that research no longer lies solely within the academy and that practitioners can become "recognised researchers (Wood 2010) and theorists (Whitehead and McNiff 2006)."

The power of teachers taking an opportunity to engage in research in their own practice, to tell the stories of their learning with honesty and authenticity, cannot be underestimated. It not only allows teachers to take action to enhance an aspect of their practice that is important to them, it also develops teachers' sense of autonomy in their classrooms while encouraging them to find their voice and use it.

Some key elements of educational action research

We will now explain how educational action research

- is a personalised process of research
- is part of a variety of action research approaches to doing research in the classroom
- is a research paradigm in its own right

A personalised process of research

Whether the research is being conducted for an accredited award or whether it is part of a personalised or school-wide continuous professional development, action research is conducted with an equal focus on rigour and validity as in any other form of research. Educational action research is not just about using an intervention to solve a problem – although such interventions are of course useful. It should be rigorous and values-based, delving into critical explorations of practice so as to lead to new insights, enhanced practice and an impetus towards creating a safer, healthier and fairer world.

The process may be individual and the findings unique to the person conducting the enquiry, as Hartog (2004) pointed out, but the study will still have educational significance and will contribute to the knowledge base of the profession (McDonagh *et al.* 2020). When you collect research information, also known as data, to show others what is happening in your classroom, or in your thinking about this, you provide explanations about your experiences. Educational action research is based on the study of the self (along with others) and it aims to capture your work in your classroom from "the multiple, complex interacting sources from which your practical knowledge has emerged" (Hamilton and Pinnegar 2014, p. 143). As teacher-researchers, we therefore draw on as many sources of data as possible and we seek to triangulate the data in order to demonstrate the trustworthiness of our accounts. Triangulation means examining your work from a number of different perspectives. It will be explained further in Chapter 4.

There is no one right form of data nor one correct data-collecting method, as you will see in later chapters. Be aware that as you seek an area to research, grounded in your wish to enhance your practice, your focus topic may shift and change as your ideas emerge. This is perfectly normal. In 2012, we wrote a report on how groups of teachers in Ireland voluntarily took responsibility for developing their own professional development programme (Glenn *et al.* 2012). They wanted to research areas of their practice that were relevant to them rather than focus on mandated enquiries dictated by top-down policy-driven agendas. During that project we saw how the selection of a research topic became a "developmental process in one's thinking rather than the naming of an object or a question to be rigorously examined" (p. 23). We further reported how "ideas emerged during the process and participants often changed their minds about the topic" (p. 23). Educational action research is significant in contexts where teachers are motivated by their own desire to engage in enhancing their practice.

Doing your own action research is then a serious intellectually responsible activity. It is far more than a mere intervention in practice. Action research has a moral basis. It is focused on people working with other people with a commitment to improving understanding and practice, and contributing to a better world. Your action research will involve more than just dipping into research, carrying out an enquiry and dipping out again. We authors, along with many others, have found that action research becomes a way of life. Rather than temporarily studying a phenomenon called "educational action research" – it is quite likely that you will, instead, actually *become* an educational action researcher.

What kind of action research?

Educational action research is part of a large variety of action research approaches to doing research in the classroom, which we will now explain. For decades, it has been generally accepted that teacher inquiry, in some form, is considered to be embedded in teaching (Clarke and Erickson 2006; Dewey 1933; Weber 1990). Indeed, Pithouse *et al.* (2009) drawing on the work of Tidwell and Fitzgerald (2004) would suggest that "teaching itself is, at heart, a kind of research" (p. 44).

There are many definitions of educational research, but these are among our favourites. According to the American Educational Research Association (nd), education research "is the scientific field of study that examines education and learning processes and the human attributes, interactions, organizations, and institutions that shape educational outcomes." Educational action research can be defined as Bassey (1999, p. 38) does as "a critical enquiry aimed at informing educational judgments in order to improve educational action."

In the current climate of performativity and its accompanying audit culture, teachers, schools and classrooms are constantly being evaluated and researched in a way that often impacts gravely on their health and well-being and sometimes yields little in the way of meaningful, transformative and sustainable new knowledge (Ball 2003; Deasy and Mannix McNamara 2016; Glenn 2021b). Some teachers are leaving the profession because of the stress that they are experiencing. Teachers in England, Wales and Northern Ireland, who were polled, cited several factors that cause stress, among them the unrealistic accountability, increased workload and lack of respect for teachers (Weale 2021).

In the past, much of the research in education that was valued by academics and educational power-holders was undertaken from an externalist stance, with the teacher and the pupils perceived as research objects, positioned under a metaphorical microscope for the edification of the so-called educational élites of research. Little attention was given to the voice of the teacher (or their pupils) and little action was taken as a result of their concerns.

Times have changed, somewhat. Large-scale research reports, undertaken from an outsider or spectator stance, still dominate the headlines on education. However, there is now, at least, an acknowledgement of the potential importance and influence of classroom research undertaken in schools, both by individual teachers and groups of teachers. Honest accounts of new learning from classroom practice and the theory generated, from the explanations provided by teachers of new insights into their practice, have begun to spring up alongside the big data research reports. For example, the research strategy of the Teaching Council of Ireland aims to "promote engagement between teachers and others engaging in research, including researchers in Higher Education Institutions" (see CROI nd). Such accounts are important because they come directly from the teachers' hearts and minds – and are not interpreted by an outside "other." They are political in their existence and in their honesty.

There is much debate about what is meant by the term "action research." Terms like "participatory action research," "collaborative action research," "emancipatory action research," "action learning," "self-study action research," among a plethora of other terms, vie for pole position in the popularity rankings. We authors believe that many of these forms of action research can support and complement one another as they inspire us practitioners to interrogate our understandings of action research so that it can help us contribute to a fairer, better world. We believe that all classroom-based research should be participatory, collaborative and emancipatory, and battles between various families of action researchers can be counter-productive. Instead, we perceive how the "convergences in which the varied kinds of knowledges embraced by action researchers" (Rowell and Feldman 2019, p. 1) can contribute to a form of action research that leads to an improved practice and a more just society. We like Kemmis' (2022, np) description of action research as a way of working which helps people to develop "their practices, their understandings of their practices, and the situations in which they live and work – to transform the work, the worker and the workplace."

We also like the term self-study as it applies to action research. "It is about me studying my practice with a view to improving it– and my understanding of it– and then making the process visible to others" (McDonagh *et al.* 2020, p. 16). We embrace these principles in our approaches to classroom research.

We support Whitehead's Living Educational Theory approach to action research as a useful model: Living Theory Action Research is an approach to action research in which:

> individual researchers generate their living-educational-theories as explanations for their educational influences in their own learning, in the learning of others and in the learning of the social formations that influence practice and understandings.

> (Whitehead 2019, p. 208)

We use the term "educational action research" to embrace these principles. It describes the ideas of applying the concepts and practices of action research to the context of education (Rauch *et al.* 2019, p. 111). We also embrace the underpinning principles of the study of the self (along with others), the cyclical nature of action research and the sharing and generation of one's living educational theory from the learning process.

As outlined earlier, we use the term "educational action research" to describe the kind of action research that we have found to be the most appropriate form of values-based research for the classroom. We perceive that educational action research embraces both the principles of self-study action research and Living Educational Theory research.

Research paradigms

There are several research paradigms or "ways of looking at the world, different assumptions about what the world is like and how we can understand or know about it" (Cohen *et al.* 2018, p. 8). While we recognise that there are multiple research paradigms, here, drawing on Bassey's work, we will refer to them briefly under three main headings: the positivist research paradigm, the interpretive research paradigm and the action research paradigm. Bassey (1990) takes some very complex ideas and explains them in easy-to-understand terms.

Bassey (1990) defines a research paradigm as

> ... a network of coherent ideas about the nature of the world and of the functions of researchers which when adhered to by a group of researchers, conditions the patterns of their thinking and underpins their research actions.

> (Bassey 1990, p. 39)

The positivist research paradigm is based on an idea of fixed realities, of the world as a rational place that makes sense and can be understood, if studied patiently for long enough. The researcher stands outside the research process and considers themselves to be objective. There is no "I" or "we" here. Discoveries about the world are presented as factual statements and propositional knowledge. The research is used to prove or disprove a hypothesis. It can be generalised, because, if replicated exactly, the findings will be the same each time. The data tends to be quantitative i.e. numerical and statistical.

Predictions can be made based on the data. This kind of research is often used in disciplines such as pharmacology, medicine, science, engineering, information technology and mathematics. It can be used in geography to analyse global or climatic phenomena, population densities and patterns of migration, etc. It is also used in education – think about PISA studies and SATs, budgets and fiscal policies, entry to third level and pupil-teacher quotas.

The interpretivist research paradigm rests on the assumption that the researcher accepts that they have a role in the research. Through asking questions, or by simply being present in a situation to observe it, the researcher can change the situation. Imagine a situation where a researcher is in a classroom observing how a teacher interacts with children who are badly behaved or struggling to learn. It is likely that the teacher, being aware of the scrutiny, will behave differently to their normal practice. Bassey (1990) asserts that, in this paradigm, the researchers cannot accept that there is a fixed reality out there separate to the knower, because reality is a human construct. People are unique and each has their own perception of reality. The data gathered in this research paradigm is most often qualitative in nature – fieldwork notes, interviews and so on, although not exclusively so. This research paradigm is prevalent in the humanities – used by historians, psychologists, anthropologists, nursing students, sociologists and social geographers. In education, this paradigm is used to look at and interpret what is happening in schools. Education students are often encouraged to read the works of these researchers. Many appear in the Education Week (2022) list of influential education scholars.

Interpretive research is valuable and important for understanding the various psychological and sociological phenomena in schools. When teachers' voices are included in the research this data will be interpreted and mediated via the researcher's perceptions. By contrast, when teacher researchers do educational action research on their own classroom practice, they tell their own story, using their own voices.

Bassey (1990) calls the third paradigm "action research." In other studies on research methods (Cohen *et al.* 2018; Al Riyami 2015), the third main paradigm is called the "critical theoretic" or "transformative" paradigm. Creswell (2007, p. 21) suggests that critical theorists believe that "research should contain an action agenda for reform that may change the lives of participants." Al Riyami (2015) says that "part of this empowerment process, which can be described as emancipation, involves research participants to problematize their current situations and decide on actions to improve them" (p. 414). She also adds that because of its ontological and epistemological assumptions, the critical theory paradigm can include many methodologies, of which the most well-known is critical action research. Cohen *et al.* (2018, p. 30) describe such research as "concerned not only with understanding a situation or phenomenon but with changing it, often with an explicit political agenda … this is reflected in the discussions of research."

Similarly, Bassey says that the action research paradigm is about actors (meaning people who are active agents) trying to improve the phenomena of their surroundings and this, he says, is what makes it differ from the other two research paradigms which are all about observing and testing in the case of positivist research, and observing and interpreting in the case of interpretative research (Bassey 1990, p. 39).

Some research textbooks use the terms "quantitative" and "qualitative" to classify research. Such a classification is not helpful as those terms refer to forms of data which we will explain in Chapter 4. "Quantitative" and "qualitative" do not explain how we understand the thinking behind research. Al Riyami (2015, p. 412) supports this view "because it implies that the main difference between research is in the type of data collected only, whereas the main difference, in fact, is at the level of ontological and epistemological assumptions."

It is important to be aware of a range of research paradigms – especially those that are relevant to your area of interest. Bassey warns that "sometimes the network of a paradigm is so strong in the minds of its practitioners that they may deny the validity of other paradigms" (Bassey 1990, p. 37). Your research should be guided by your own epistemological and ontological beliefs and about what it is you want to discover. You should use these brief descriptions of the three main paradigms that we have outlined briefly here (as well as the many other paradigms that exist in research literature) to help guide, clarify and organise your thinking about your research (Cohen *et al.* 2018).

The importance of educational action research

We move on now to look at the bigger picture outside your classroom. The main headings under which we invite you to consider the possible importance of conducting educational action research are theory, practice, praxis, expanding teacher professional voice and empowerment.

Theory, practice and praxis

In academia, for many years the sciences were valued above the humanities. Propositional knowledge and the idea of generalisation and replication were thought to ensure rigour and trustworthiness in the research process. Thus the positivist research paradigm gained dominance over "softer" forms of research. Schön (1995) described this hierarchy of academics versus practitioners, when he referred to the ivory towers of academia and the swampy lowlands of practice-based research. There was a traditional theory-practice divide that was in some ways ameliorated by the arrival of action research and practice-based research.

That hierarchical division between practitioner and researcher is one that is still contested and interrogated by those of us who engage in educational action research. As we undertake educational action research in our practice, we are teachers who are also researchers who generate validated theory from our practice (McNiff and Whitehead 2006). This is a challenging concept for many who feel that teachers' research into their practice needs to be interpreted by academic outsiders before it is considered to be adequately authoritative. It is ironic that this is still the case in the 2020s when teachers in most jurisdictions not only learn action research skills as part of their teacher-education programmes, they also *do* research in their practice as part of their accreditation. We teacher-researchers have some work to do in this slow battle against archaic academic norms. We hope that by reading this book, you will gain the confidence to do your research in your classroom and have your voice heard as you share the story of your learning with others.

The term *praxis* is one that crops up frequently in educational action research literature. Praxis refers to the interplay between reflection and action, which is informed, not only by questioning and critique, but also by dialogue with others. Its aim is that practice, which in this case is probably teaching, becomes a critically informed action (Carr and Kemmis 1986) that is undertaken by practitioners aiming to "transform their work and society at large" (Torres and Mercado 2004, p. 61). Kemmis defines praxis thus: "'Educational praxis,' therefore, may be understood in two ways: first, as educational action that is morally-committed and informed by traditions in a field ('right conduct'), and second, as 'history-making educational action'" (Kemmis 2012, p. 894). Therefore, the principles of praxis underpin our thinking in educational action research as we critically reflect on our work; try to learn more about it; query the assumptions we make and aim towards improving both our practice and the world in which we live.

Teacher voice – teacher as professional developing a researcherly disposition

Educational action research provides teachers and other educational practitioners with a methodology that is perfectly suited, both ontologically and epistemologically, to carrying out enquiries in a classroom or other educational institutional setting. The paradigm accepts the uniqueness of each individual's perception and the tentative and evolving nature of knowledge. Along with the moral underpinning of it being research *with* others rather than research *on* others, each action researcher accepts that their research is invitational and collaborative, grounded in values of social justice and equity. Teachers have long been research aware and research-informed, but now they are equipped to be research active. Lingard and Renshaw (2010) spoke about the need for education practitioners and policy-makers to develop a researcherly disposition. We authors took this concept a step further and advocated that people working in education might develop an "action researcherly disposition" (Sullivan *et al.* 2016, p. 69).

Researching one's own practice enables teachers to develop a sense of agency and to display accountability for their own actions. It lessens their reliance on being passive receivers of others' knowledge. It allows for their voices to be heard and valued. It empowers them to address their particular and unique concerns and to examine, problematise and enhance their own practice. In McDonagh *et al.* (2020) we argue that researching one's own practice can contribute to an improved sense of agency, a stronger teacher identity and enhanced well-being. Enquiring into one's own practice can be an emancipatory and transformational process, involving, as it does, the concepts of collegiality, collaboration, dialogue and open-mindedness. Engaging in educational action research can lead to knowledge generation and developing a personal educational theory. The interplay between research, practice, theory and action lies at the heart of educational action research. According to Al Riyami (2015, p. 415), "when a person's daily life is based on action and reflection, emancipation and amelioration can be achieved, and a better life can be lived."

Empowerment

It would be incorrect to maintain that engaging in educational action research has a direct impact on a teacher's sense of empowerment and autonomy. There is, however, a connection between doing educational research in one's practice and the sense of taking control of, and doing something about, one aspect of your practice. This is important for teachers who work in a system that expects high performance and allows little room for teachers to think for themselves. When practitioners focus on their values, learn more about what is important for them in their lives and begin to work towards aligning their outside life with the values they hold (Chatterjee 2022), they begin to lead a more meaningful and intentional life, it can lead to a greater sense of contentment.

Conclusion

We hope that this chapter has helped you to put in place some of the necessary practical and theoretical foundations for beginning an educational action research project. In this chapter we have outlined the preliminary activities that can be taken to kickstart an educational action research project in terms of initial tasks, reflective tasks and writing tasks. We have drawn examples from practising teachers' research accounts to highlight how they experienced educational action research to enhance their practice and how teachers can gain new insights into their understanding of their practice. The chapter has also outlined briefly the main elements that pertain to educational action research.

In the next chapter we will explore how you might begin the more formal aspects of an educational action research project.

Additional reading suggestions

Greene, M. (1984) 'How we think about the craft of teaching', *Teachers College Record*, 86(1), 55–67. Available https://maxinegreene.org/uploads/library/how_we_think_craft.pdf (Open Access)

McNiff, J. (n.d.) *Action Research for Professional Development*, available http://jeanmcniff.com/ ar-booklet.asp [accessed 12 April 2022]. (Open Access)

Petrarca, D. and Van Nuland, S. (2020) 'Initial teacher education practicum 2.0' in Kitchen, J., Berry, A., Bullock, S.M., Crowe, A.R., Taylor, M., Guðjónsdóttir, H., and Thomas, L. eds., *International Handbook of Self-study of Teaching and Teacher Education Practices*, Singapore: Springer, 1103–1130.

Suggested resources

The following are short courses on general action research which can be accessed free of charge:

- *Action Research and Evaluation on Line (AREOL)* is available in two formats, both free. The 15-week public email course is offered twice a year as a public service by ALARA, the Action Learning Action Research Association Inc. or through video tutorials with Bob Dick at http://www.aral.com.au/areol/areolind.html
- *Action Research Tutorials* at the Centre of Collaborative Action Research with Margaret Riel at https://www.actionresearchtutorials.org/

- *Teachers as Researchers – Improving Classroom Practice through Action Research* by EUAcademy at https://academy.europa.eu/courses/teachers-as-researchers-improving-classroom-practice-through-action-research-1658151350

Open access journals

- *Directory of Open Access Journals* (DOAJ) https://doaj.org/ (All 18,000 journals are open-access - but not all pertain to education).
- *Educational Action Research Journal* (Some articles are Open Access). https://www.tandfonline.com/journals/reac20
- *Educational Journal of Living Theories* (EJOLTs) https://www.ejolts.net/
- *Teaching and Teacher Education* https://www.journals.elsevier.com/teaching-and-teacher-education/open-access-articles
- *99 Excellent Open Access Journals for Educators* https://www.onlinecollege.org/2009/11/11/100-excellent-open-access-journals-for-educators/

2 Getting started: Asking "Why am I concerned or interested?"

In this chapter we outline how you might begin the more formal aspects of your research. Your research project can be about anything you want to change or enhance in your practice. It can be about something you would like to celebrate. It can also be about just trying to understand your practice at a deeper level. You might address questions like "What are my concerns? What am I interested in?" and "Why am I concerned? Why am I interested?" (Whitehead and McNiff 2006; Sullivan et al. 2016). Your responses to these questions will form the basis of your research and as you refine them and hone them, they will help to establish the focus of your research.

Your research journey will be as individual as you are. You bring your own unique values, beliefs and identity to your teaching and now you will find how you can bring your beliefs and identity to doing educational action research, which will be grounded in your values. Whitehead reminds us: "In creating their own living-theory methodology, an individual includes the unique constellation of values that they use to give meaning and purpose to their existence" (2018, p. 82).

This chapter offers

- suggestions on some tasks to undertake as you get started on the formal aspects of your research project
- insights on how other teachers and student teachers learned to articulate their values as they became critically reflective
- an exploration of the purpose of asking "Why am I concerned or interested?"

Section 1: Tasks to undertake as you get started on the more formal aspects of your research project

Ongoing tasks

Reflective journal

Continue to take time to pause and think, and to add to your reflective journal. Re-read earlier entries and see if your thinking has changed. Make note of these changes and of new ideas that come to you as you re-read your journal entries. Be critical and question assumptions that you might have made about education.

DOI: 10.4324/9781003288183-3

Values

Continue to examine your values. Ask yourself why they might be of importance to you. Check to see if there are occasions when you see your values being enacted in your practice - or not.

This is an important activity because as you begin to see what is important to you, you will find a focus for your research. It will also help you to track your new learning in your journal and help you to establish the validity of your claim to new knowledge about your practice.

Reading

Professional reading is an essential part of the research process. It is something that you will need to make time for. It will be important too, that you use this time wisely. You should read widely around education but specifically around your area of interest. You will need to take notes and to read critically, which means that you should question the views that you come across in the literature, rather than simply taking them at face value.

If you have a supervisor, they may point you towards initial readings that they feel will spark your interest or that may be seminal readings in your field of research. Take this advice seriously: read the papers or books and be prepared to discuss them with your supervisor or critical friend. This reading can often ignite or renew a passion for your teaching as you play with the ideas that are presented to you. Use the list of references at the end of the book or paper to extend your reading list. Reading articles with which you agree can animate your own passion for the topic, but it is also important to read some articles with which you might disagree. These, too, even though you may disagree with them, can awaken your creativity, and develop in you a more critical stance. It is a good idea to make notes as you read. Ask yourself questions like "Has my thinking changed because of my reading? How?", "Do I agree with the author or disagree? Why?", "Has my reading helped me to articulate the ideas that I hold? How?", "Have I seen anything with fresh eyes? What?" These notes will help you as you engage with your critical reflection on your practice. They will also help to interrogate your own assumptions about your teaching and about education in general, as they become the first draft of a literature review chapter in a research report.

Take note of your readings by making a list of their titles, as well as the names of the authors, year of publication and place of publication. Many researchers like to use citation management tools such as *EndNote, Mendeley, RefWorks,* or *Zotero,* for example, to help them keep track of articles they have read, but others prefer to just write a list. You will now be beginning to itemise works to contribute to the reference list at the end of your report. The works listed in it appear in alphabetical order according to the author's surname. If a specific referencing convention has not been recommended to you, there are many freely available on university websites. Choose one and adhere to it.

Talking and sharing ideas

Research in practice is never done alone - it is always done with others. Even though your research will be focused on yourself and your thinking, and in writing your report, you will use "I", this should not be a selfish or egotistical "I" (Whitehead 2018). Instead, your focus should be on "I" in collaboration with others. Sharing your tentative ideas with critical friends and validation groups from the outset is an important aspect of educational action research. This ensures that you engage in a cooperative and dialogical process of research. We will explain validation groups later in Chapter 5.

Choose your critical friends wisely. As explained previously, your critical friends should be fairly familiar with your work setting (they may be other teachers), and they should be supportive of you and your research. They would also need to be stringent and be ready to be critical of any woolly thinking you might present to them. As you and your critical friends talk to one another and as you share your most current ideas through dialogue, you are already showing how you are interrogating your assumptions and becoming a critically re-flective teacher. It might be helpful to reread Baskerville and Goldblatt (2009). Citing Schuk and Russell (2005), they suggest that the critiquing aspect of critical friendship needs to develop sensitively and slowly. They suggest establishing protocols for giving feedback on aspects of practice. These protocols need to be revisited over time, they add "[to develop] the language and the demeanour to enhance feedback and effect changes in behaviour and approaches" (Baskerville and Goldblatt 2009, p. 218).

Reflecting tasks

Ask yourself "What am I concerned about?" or "What am I interested in?" or "What would I like to find out more about?"

When you decide to engage in research in your practice, one of the first steps you take is to think about what is of the utmost importance to you. Very often it is something that is puzzling you or is causing you concern, and may therefore appear to be a problem. You might then ask yourself "how do I improve my practice?" (Whitehead and McNiff 2006, p. 19). It could also be something in your everyday practice which interests you or something about which you might like to learn more. "Indeed, it can be an area [of your practice] that you feel should be cele-brated" (McDonagh *et al.* 2016, p. 40), and you might like to investigate why this is important. Your area of concern often becomes more apparent as you talk to colleagues, look at entries in your reflective journal and check for recurring or repeated themes.

Ask yourself "Why am I concerned?" or "Why is this aspect of my work important to me?" "What connection can you make between your answers and your values?"

These are more difficult questions because they delve into the values and beliefs you hold. For example, your dissatisfaction with how you teach literacy may stem from the values you hold around fairness, access to education and social justice. We discuss how you might address these "Why?" questions in greater detail in Section 2 of this chapter.

You can examine and explore any of several areas of your practice. You might consider organising these possibilities into the sections as outlined in Figure 2.1, in order to arrive at a potential research question or area of concern. Remember the concern does not have to be grounded in a negative – you can also ask yourself "What am I doing well, and how might I do it better?"

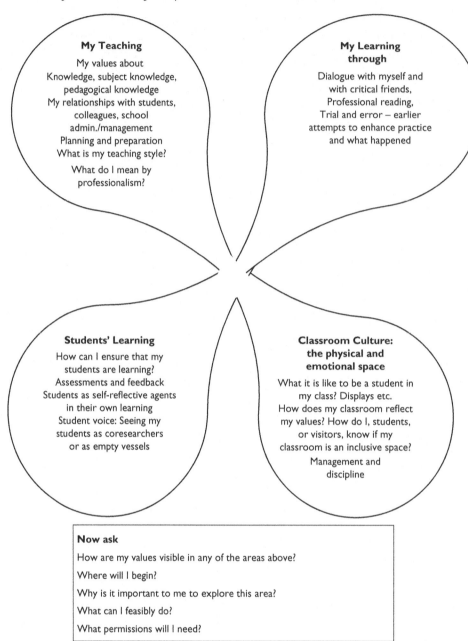

My Teaching

My values about
Knowledge, subject knowledge,
pedagogical knowledge
My relationships with students,
colleagues, school
admin./management
Planning and preparation
What is my teaching style?

What do I mean by
professionalism?

**My Learning
through**

Dialogue with myself and
with critical friends,
Professional reading,
Trial and error – earlier
attempts to enhance practice
and what happened

Students' Learning

How can I ensure that my
students are learning?
Assessments and feedback
Students as self-reflective agents
in their own learning
Student voice: Seeing my
students as coresearchers
or as empty vessels

**Classroom Culture:
the physical and
emotional space**

What it is like to be a student in
my class? Displays etc.
How does my classroom reflect
my values? How do I, students,
or visitors, know if my
classroom is an inclusive space?
Management and
discipline

Now ask

How are my values visible in any of the areas above?

Where will I begin?

Why is it important to me to explore this area?

What can I feasibly do?

What permissions will I need?

Figure 2.1 What area attracts me most as a focus for my research?

In Figure 2.1, you can see a selection of areas of practice that can be examined and explored. Some of these may be located in the microcosm of your everyday classroom; others may be more to do with philosophical ideas around the macro or wider world of education. It might be helpful to realise that you can view your practice through several lenses. Brookfield (2017, p. 61) describes how, when trying on clothes in a shop, we often have multiple mirrors that show us back views and side views. He relates this experience to critical reflection and speaks about how "we need to be able to see ourselves from unfamiliar angles." Describing possible lenses of critical reflection – students' eyes, colleagues' perceptions, personal experience, theory – he suggests that "they provide four different ways for teachers to look at what they do … [and] when we try to build these lenses into our teaching we do better work" (Brookfield 2017, p. 77).

Think about any assumptions you might have made about teaching and education

As you step into your classroom for the first time, either as a student or as a teacher and educator, you come with certain assumptions that you have made about schools, teaching and classrooms. Very often they are embedded in your thinking and you tend to resist questioning them (Brookfield 2017). However, as you become critically reflective, you should try to identify the assumptions that you make about your work so that you can better understand your actions as a teacher. This is part of your work as a teacher/researcher.

Can you connect your ideas with working for a more equitable democratic society?

Action research is not just about simply undertaking an intervention in the classroom, it is also about transformation, growth and sustainable change, and is "committed to change for social and environmental justice" (Ledwith 2017, p. 56). Because your research is grounded in your values, you may fulfil your commitment to your values by ensuring a more just and equitable educational experience for your students. We discuss this in more detail in Section 3 of this chapter.

Imagining

This is a good opportunity to play with ideas. Pithouse *et al.* (2009, p. 47) remind us that "Mucking about, making mistakes, changing one's mind are not viewed as shameful, but rather as learning opportunities that can provoke creative solutions." Take time now to pause and imagine how you might like your life or your workplace to be, explore the possibilities that lie within you as a teacher and think about how you might begin to achieve this. Imagine too how you might best address your area of interest or concern. What strategy or plan of action might you consider?

Writing tasks

As you work through these tasks, they will become practice writing and as you redraft them throughout the research process, they will contribute to a final written report.

Try answering the following questions, using Figure 2.1 to help you.

What are my concerns/areas of interest regarding my practice and how are these connected with my values?

Why am I concerned/interested specifically in relation to values and practice?

What might I do about it?

How will I establish that I am enhancing my practice and living more closely to my values? This may become draft writing for a methodology section of a research report.

Choose a research article that you have read and that outlines a current area of debate in the field of education.

> Describe it briefly and write about how it influences your thinking about your area of interest.

> Explain why you agree/disagree with it. This may become draft writing for a literature review section of a research report.

We have synopsised these tasks in Figure 2.2. These tasks are not a definitive list, they are merely the tasks that we authors find useful. Please modify these for your own use.

Ongoing Tasks	Yes	No	Under way
Continue to write a reflective journal			
Reflecting on and naming values	—	—	—
Reading	—	—	—
Talking and sharing your ideas			
Thinking tasks	Yes	No	Under way
Ask yourself 'What am I concerned about?'	—	—	
Ask yourself 'Why am I concerned?'	—	—	
Connecting to your values	—	—	
Question assumptions	—	—	—
Can you connect your ideas with working for a more equitable society?	—	—	—
Imagine possibilities	—	—	—
Writing Tasks	Yes	No	Under way
Imagine how you might best address your area of interest or concern (As draft writing for a methodology section)	—	—	—
Continue writing about your area of interest. (As draft writing for a methodology and literature review section)	—	—	—
Ongoing Tasks	*Yes*	*No*	*Under way*
Continue to write a reflective journal			
Reflecting on and naming values	—	—	—
Reading	—	—	—
Talking and sharing your ideas			

Figure 2.2 Tasks to help you get started on the more formal aspects of your research project

Section 2: How teachers and student teachers articulate their values

Values give meaning to our lives. In this book we are focusing on the values that inform our professional lives, but often, our personal values are interwoven with our professional ones. In our working lives, the animating principles that govern our personal lives might also apply, such as those that help us to make decisions in our everyday lives about who to trust, how to behave, the life choices we make and the stances we take. They are all informed by our values, and by the assumptions we hold. These in turn are influenced by our own personal history, our identity and sense of self.

When you think about your work, what comes to mind first? What are you proud of? What are you unsure of? What do you feel could perhaps be improved? These feelings and thoughts are firmly underpinned by the values you hold. In this section of the chapter, we expand on values and critical reflection, and discuss their importance both for practice and research. We draw on stories taken from teachers' and student teachers' educational action research.

Because educational action research is values-based and values-led, we link it to the values we hold. Whitehead (2018) reminds us that education is a value-laden practical activity. He suggests that "these values, which are embodied in our practice, are often referred to in terms such as freedom, justice, democracy (Peters 1966), and 'love and productive work (Fromm 1960)'" (Whitehead 2018, p. 14). One of the strengths of action research is that it is deeply personal and contextualised, "drawing on the values and beliefs of the researcher, and challenging him/her to reconcile those values and beliefs with practice" (McAteer 2013, p. 33). So, for example, if your area of interest is students' well-being, that might be drawn from your values around care and respect. Right through the research process, you will be looking for data to show that you are enhancing your practice or gaining insight into it and living more closely to your values of care and respect.

Living contradictions

In his seminal paper written in 1989, Jack Whitehead introduces the idea of experiencing oneself as "a living contradiction." By this he means that we can hold values dearly while simultaneously denying them in our practice. We authors have all experienced this phenomenon in different ways and have written about it (see Sullivan *et al.* 2016; Glenn *et al.* 2017 and McDonagh *et al.* 2020). Over the years many have described this idea in a variety of ways and in a variety of research fields. Coghlan and Brannick (2005, p. 135), for example, describe it as "value tensions" when action research is being conducted within the researcher's organisation. "Value conflicts" is how Valutis and Rubin (2016, p. 11) and Muñoz-Arce and Rubilar-Donoso (2021, p. 11) describe where personal and professional values clash in social workers' practices. In your educational action research this phenomenon may not occur at a conceptual level only but as a real living dilemma. Leitch (2018, p. 162) finds the term "living the paradox" helpful in explaining the contradictions in her ongoing practice as she tries "to succeed as an academic researcher within those boundaries imposed by policy and political imperatives in modern UK higher education ... ." She references the term to the Nobel prize-winning poet Seamus Heaney (1984) where he tells of his ongoing "living the paradox" as he questioned "how to be socially responsible and creatively free" (Leitch 2018, p. 162).

On Jack Whitehead's webpage www.actionresearch.net there are many other examples of practitioner researchers experiencing themselves as living contradictions. Here are some simple caricatures to illustrate what we mean:

- Tom is a school principal who values teacher agency, yet finds it difficult, as a school leader, to trust his staff and to delegate
- Irene is a post-primary teacher who values independent thought in her students yet finds herself compelled to give them rote learning work in order to equip them for written exams
- Jim is a primary teacher who values creativity and freedom in education yet finds himself giving templates for art to his 30 kindergarten students
- Abbie is a lecturer who values action research but who works in a college devoted to quantitative research
- Alex is a student teacher who is passionate about giving pupils the opportunity to express themselves. On his teaching placement, his mentor/cooperating teacher dislikes "noise and chat"

Can you see the inherent dilemma in holding values and being unable or unwilling to live them in practice? Can you also see that the tensions inherent within each of these scenarios might contain potential for a great piece of action research?

Let's now take a little time to examine the values that might inform our professional lives as educators.

Simply, these can broadly be broken down into two main sets: (i) our views and ideas about knowledge: what knowledge is; the different forms of knowledge; knowledge acquisition; knowledge generation; knowledge dissemination; who counts as a knower and who says, etc. These are called *epistemological* values - or values about ways of knowing. Then there are (ii) our views about our place in the world and our relationships - how we see others, and how we see ourselves in relation to them. These are called *ontological* values - or values about ways of being. Both these sets of values influence how we work, and who we are in our classrooms, practice settings, lecture halls and staff rooms. You could say they form the basis of our *methodological* values - values about ways of working and researching.

A caricature: Maggie believes firmly in a didactic approach to teaching. She relies heavily on the textbooks and has strong views on the transmission of knowledge, rote learning, knowledge retrieval, silence in classrooms (student silence - the talk is mostly hers) and summative assessment. Her approach is largely monological. She doesn't hold with all these new-fangled ideas about dialogical approaches and constructivist or student-centred learning. She feels she's not there to be the students' friend and is largely ignorant of their lives outside of the classroom. She teaches as she was taught - using a whole class approach - what Lortie (1975) called "the apprenticeship of observation." Those students who do well, she feels, do so because of her good teaching and their own hard work. Those who fall behind, she believes, are lazy and uninterested - not her problem.

This caricature shows us that Maggie's epistemological values are that knowledge is largely information to be inserted into students' brains by the teacher; that learning is a matter of memorising facts, and that success depends on students working hard and being able to regurgitate these facts for exams. In 1854, in his novel *Hard Times*, Dickens recognised this kind of utilitarian education when he wrote about Mr Gradgrind. Paulo Freire, writing in the 1970s, called it "the banking model of education" (2005, p. 71). Some would argue that some of our more recent efforts at pivoting to online teaching fell into this category too where "knowledge is thus perceived as information that can be packaged and transferred to others" (Sullivan *et al.* 2022, p. 8). This concept of education, Freire (2005) argued, dehumanises students and oppresses them. In classrooms where this model prevails, he argued, students are treated as things or objects. They are considered to be empty vessels who sit and wait so as to "download"/receive, file and store the deposits of information (Freire 2005).

From the caricature above we can see that Maggie's values influence her teaching style, her pedagogical relationships and her understanding of education in general. Teachers like Maggie may not intend to oppress or dehumanise their students - they are often hardworking diligent people who would probably be horrified at this interpretation of their work.

Playing with ideas

1   Reflect on your own views on knowledge. What do YOU believe? How does learning happen, in your opinion? Who, do you think, is a learner, and who is a knower, in your classroom? Your answers may give you some clues about your epistemological values.

2   Try to envisage or imagine a contrasting caricature to the one outlined above - one that perhaps shows a teacher who has more problem-posing or critical views of knowledge, and whose pedagogical relationships are visible in a more dialogical approach.

3   Think now about your relationship with the students in your classroom or practice setting. How do you view them? Is each student an "it" or an "object" to be controlled and coerced, as Freire described? Or are they individuals, just like you are, each one unique, and as deserving of dignity and respect as you feel yourself to be?

How you think about your students - the people with whom you work - will give you some insights into your ontological values. Be very honest with yourself.

You have now begun the process of critically reflecting on your practice.

How some teacher-researchers engaged with critical reflection

Ruth is a post-primary teacher. In the final year of her undergraduate degree, as an education student heading out on placement, she began learning about action research and particularly, self-study action research. Here is her account now as she looks back at her work then and how it has impacted on her ever since.

> I was introduced to action research during my undergraduate degree. Initially as with all assessments within a busy degree it was just one more element, another box to tick and another submission to be made. I gave it my full effort at the time purely because my tutor was so passionate about the concept of action research. She placed particular emphasis on critical reflection and the benefits this had to a teacher's practice, but honestly at the time I didn't understand what critical reflection was. Looking back on my notes I have MUST CRITICALLY REFLECT highlighted on numerous pages.
>
> I took a very simplistic route with the idea of action research at the time, nothing overly complicated. I posed a question I had regarding my teaching and whether or not it was actually effective, and I implemented my research during the normal course of my timetabled classes. I can keenly remember the first few classes, some students responded immediately and others not at all. I couldn't stop thinking about how to proceed with the students it had worked with and how to get those students who hadn't responded to respond in any way at all. I moved and changed my approaches, I applied different questions to some students and different handouts and gave more time to other students. Some changes worked and some did not. I started to scribble down what was working and what was not. Yellow post-it notes everywhere! (I eventually put them all in a notebook for myself.) After a number of classes I realised that there were probably other steps involved in reflecting on my practice that I needed to look at and complete. However, to my surprise when I checked my lecture slides, I was already doing them. I was critically reflecting without "making myself" critically reflect, it was flowing and happening. No big steps, just action, reaction, observation and reflection in a circular motion so it went on and on, changing as it needed to.

Ruth devises a personal "post-its" form of journaling which suits her and her work and develops it into a verifiable form of critical reflection. While she was studying herself in her practice with a view to improving it – and her understanding of it – she then makes "the process visible to others" (McDonagh *et al.* 2020, p. 16). Ruth's thinking in the section above is from her years as a student teacher. In the next sections we see how Ruth uses critical reflection as a classroom teacher.

> Key areas of my class just weren't working and that was simple to see in interactions with students. Once I trialled something new, then observed, reflected and changed certain areas, the classes got better. Not all of them but there was movement, I wasn't

stuck in one spot. Classes either changed and improved or I asked for advice, I talked to other teachers, to friends and retried or got rid of my teaching approaches. Soon school placement ended. My notebook was full of post-its. So much of what I had been doing or thinking wasn't effective. I now had 20 more questions about me as a teacher, about the ideas I had on teaching, about the ideas I had of my students, about me. I complained to my tutor that it hadn't worked like I had hoped because while my first question was answered I now had more questions, so many more, she laughed and told me I was going in the right direction. (She was right, it turns out.)

In the five years that followed, Ruth's teaching experience broadened. She taught in tough schools and worked with non-governmental organisations (NGOs) on education projects for students from disadvantaged backgrounds. So, what happened about her critical reflection?

I no longer have post-its or even a notebook, but I reflect every day and I have questions every day. I question aspects within myself and my practice, within my interactions with students and education workers. I question my assumptions and my wording, my thoughts and my heart. A colleague recently asked me how I work with people who are so difficult without making assumptions and letting it affect my work and the way I interact with individuals and groups. I told her that I make assumptions every single time I enter a room or meet a new person or hold a conversation but now instead of holding onto that thought I reflect. I critically reflect and check where that thought is coming from and why. I have a think about where that individual or group is coming from and why they are acting as they are and why I am responding or feeling as I am and maybe what I can do to change, help or move on. Every day I use this unassuming critical little tool. Without it I would have held so many assumptions unknown to myself, I would have been cross with many students and blamed them, I would have found work tough. I would have stopped teaching for them and started teaching for a job. I use it at work, in meetings, with colleagues, with easy and tough students, at home, with my children. It has moved endlessly and easily around my life. When feeling uncomfortable feelings or even happy ones I have a think as to why, what caused it and how to capture or remove that and then I go again.

Looking back on her various experiences of using critical reflection, Ruth says that she has realised there are three important areas of critical reflection.

The most crucial part of critical reflection is ensuring that while you are reflecting you don't take the easy route, blame something else and move on. You question yourself and sit in the uncomfortable space for a while. For me, sometimes maybe it's my thoughts and actions, maybe I have just been wrong (my husband loves to hear me say that). Secondly, critically reflecting takes time, something happens, or you start to reflect,

> and you just don't have the answers or cannot see the fire through the smoke at that particular time. When this has happened, I let it lie and I hold onto the question and as time moves on, further actions take place, then suddenly I may see that whilst reflecting on something completely different I realise a link or a gap that I had not noticed before and there the answers lie. So time for me is a big element. Lastly, you must be gentle. I am notoriously hard on myself. I try to remember when reflecting that not everything is within my power and not all problems are my own alone.
>
> I am currently completing a Masters in Equality studies. Critical reflection is my right hand. I haven't got it right in all aspects, nor do I imagine I ever will, but I strive to improve, change and move forward. Like Maxine Greene – "I AM NOT YET" (Pinar, 1998).

Ruth has shown that beginning the process of investigating her own practice is rooted in critical reflection. This can be a painful process, and she has learned to be gentle with herself while maintaining rigour and authenticity because she recognises the value that it has for her own professional development and sense of identity as a teacher.

Now we look at Aideen, who is a post-primary teacher currently teaching in the UAE (United Arab Emirates). The aim of her self-study action research was to develop her own practice and understanding in the area of student self-esteem in order to try to become a more inclusive practitioner. Like Ruth she was introduced to self-study action research during her undergraduate teacher education course, prior to going on teaching placement.

Aideen's reflections:

> During this action research I investigated the impact that I, as the teacher, could have on the self-esteem of my students. Throughout the course the importance of self-esteem for students was highlighted so I wanted to investigate ways of improving my practice to create a learning environment conducive to developing students' self-esteem. This research study became a vital part of my educational practice. While I discovered methods of improving students' self-esteem, which positively impacted them and improved my abilities as a teacher, I also discovered the significance of researching oneself in one's practice. It provided a way to ensure that I was not becoming a living contradiction in my practice and that my actions were in line with my educational philosophies and values. Self-study has highlighted the importance of investigating my own practice to ensure that what I think I am doing and the desired outcome of my actions is actually what is happening.
>
> Without conducting this research, I would not be aware of the strengths and weaknesses in my practice. This was an important factor to learn because even though my actions were informed by educational theories or research, self-study helped me to identify what was happening in my own situation. I would not have improved my critical thinking and reflective practice. As a result of this positive experience with self-study in my undergraduate degree I have taken the time to investigate the impact of my own

> *actions throughout my teaching career. This has impacted my educational progress as this process assisted me in identifying strengths in my practice that I could share with colleagues or identify areas of improvement. I would use the information from this process to inform my continuous professional development.*

Aideen demonstrates with clarity here how educational action research has been not only transformative for her but is also sustainable and a life-long process. She began her process of professional learning through educational action research in her undergraduate teaching program. She has continued on her journey of professional learning through her research in her practice in the intervening years:

> *One of the most important lessons I learned from my self-study was the ability to be open in all aspects of my professional practice – open to the feedback from my critical friends in the process, open to themes and ideas that were being identified in the investigation both positive and negative. This concept of openness that was promoted through self-study has positively impacted my educational progress. As I have worked in schools in The United Kingdom, Ireland and the UAE this openness allowed me to adapt quickly to new curricula, contexts, methodologies and research. It has improved my practice as I am now more open to feedback, to engaging with new research within different contexts and finding new and innovative ways to improve my practice that is suited to the needs of my students.*
>
> *Overall, my self-study has inspired my passion for research and instilled in me the value of education as a life-long process. This has encouraged me to complete further research as I recently completed an MSc in Psychological Science and I will be starting another self-study as I am currently completing an MA in Leadership in Education.*

Aideen identifies the importance of her research for her continuous professional development. Not only has she addressed her concerns, engaged in critical research, but she now also explains how she learned the importance of being open to dialogue, change and critique – ideas we will discuss in Section 3 of this chapter.

Section 3: What are my concerns and interests? Why am I concerned or interested? How are these questions linked to the educational action research process?

In this section of the chapter, we will explore why we might address questions such as:

What are my concerns and interests and why am I concerned or interested?
Critical reflection – how is this linked to the values that I hold?
What is the importance of reflexivity and dialogue?
How can classroom educational action research lead to transformation?

What are my concerns/areas of interest and why am I concerned or interested?

When undertaking research in their practice, the first two questions teacher researchers ask themselves are "What am I concerned about?" and "Why am I concerned?" according to McNiff and Whitehead (2011, p. 9). They suggest the following questions contribute to a research cycle:

What is my concern?
Why am I concerned?
How do I show the situation as it is and as it develops?
What can I do about it? What will I do about it?
How do I test the validity of my claims to knowledge?
How do I check that any conclusions I come to are reasonably fair and accurate?
How do I modify my ideas and practices in light of the evaluation? (Adapted from Whitehead 1989; McNiff and Whitehead 2011, p. 9)

We authors felt that in asking "What is my concern?" there was an implied negativity in the assumption that there was some problem with one's practice. Sometimes teachers like to investigate areas that are of interest to them or aspects of their practice that excite them, as well as exploring what is of concern to them. Consequently, we modified these questions slightly (Sullivan *et al.* 2016) by suggesting that along with questions to do with improvement, we could expand the idea to include the notion of enhancement or celebration. Examples of such questions might be "What is my area of interest? What would I like to celebrate in my practice?" and "Why?"

By attempting to answer questions like "What is my concern/area of interest?" you are beginning to find a focus for your research and imagining a research question. As you start to reflect on what your main area of concern or interest might be, you can become overwhelmed by the myriad of issues that enter your consciousness and cause concern for you. Bear in mind that you are already probably a good, conscientious teacher but that, now, you are striving to be even better. Try to prioritise your areas of concern according to importance and according to the values that inspire your life in education. Discuss your ideas with critical friends because sometimes friends might have a good insight into what is important in your life too. It is a good idea now, to comb through your reflective journal and check for topics that arise frequently. These are indicators of what might be of concern or interest to you. As you begin to find a focus for your research, you might refine your area of concern and narrow it down to a focal area for investigation. It is advisable to choose an area that you might be able to do something about, given the limitations of your own situation and the timeframe available to you.

As you investigate *what* your concerns and areas of interest are, you also need to investigate *why* you are concerned and interested in a specific area of your practice. Both questions are intertwined.

Addressing the reasons you are concerned or interested in an area of your practice can be a challenging exercise. The process is usually linked with your own belief system and the values you hold. We will outline next how you might begin to address the question "Why am I concerned/interested?"

Critical reflection – how is this linked to the values that I hold?

Now we are going to explore how to become critically reflective. You become critically reflective when you begin to question your everyday habits and practices. You can ask yourself why you do what you do. McNiff and Whitehead (2009) explain it well:

> 'Critical' in action research never implies negative criticism. It refers to the process of critique, when we problematise issues and unpack them for hidden meanings and assumptions.
>
> McNiff and Whitehead (2009, p.150)

As you problematise issues, you begin to question the influences of power that originate outside the classroom and influence practice inside it, as well as those unfair power dynamics that exist within classrooms and staff rooms, without any apparent external influence.

Brookfield (2017) suggests that we should unearth unfair power dynamics and examples of hegemony in the classroom when we become critically reflective. He suggests that as critically reflective practitioners, we examine assumptions we make regarding teacher power. Brookfield also draws on Gramsci's (1971) ideas around hegemony. He suggests that we should also seek examples of hegemony in which "ideas, structures, and actions that benefit a small minority in power are viewed by the majority of people as ... working for their own good" (Brookfield 2017, p. 16). His suggestion around utilising the lenses of the students' eyes; colleagues' perceptions; personal experiences and theory when we examine our practice in a critical manner, helps us seek out the assumptions we naturally make about our practice and to challenge any issues of power and hegemony that we encounter.

When you do an action research project, you do it to enhance, celebrate or learn more about practice. As you become more familiar with and critical of your practice, you become more autonomous and confident about it. By asking "Why am I concerned about or interested in this?" you also learn to place your practice in a broader context of your influence on society and to investigate how you might make the world a better place.

The importance of reflexivity and dialogue

By critically reflecting on your reflections, you will see how far you have travelled and how differently you now think compared with when you began. This is a feature of action research that we call "reflexivity." Robertson (2000) suggested that reflexivity is integral to the process of action research.

Robertson proposes that in order to arrive at self-awareness the researcher should ask and answer questions such as: How has this research transformed me? Has it penetrated deeply into my daily life and work? Has it varied my self-awareness of my work as a teacher and researcher? She argues that the knowledge of the world cannot be advanced apart from teachers' own knowledge of themselves and their position in the social world.

We authors see this as values-laden educational action research. Like Robertson, we recognise that all the data we gather is interpreted and filtered through our own existing information, beliefs and experiences.

The researcher is constantly being transformed through keeping reflective diaries/journals, sifting through the data, re-reading the literature to make new decisions as to the next action, involved in continual dialogue with their own reflections, with critical friends and other participants, "all of the time becoming more aware of themselves and the processes they are utilising" (Robertson 2000, p. 131). Whitehead suggests that reflexivity occurs when we seek to find our values being enacted in our work. He says (2018, p. 142) "By reflexivity, I mean we clarify and communicate the ontological values we use to give our lives meaning and purpose … ."

Dialogue

You may notice that throughout this book, we recommend reading, writing and engaging in dialogue as ongoing tasks for the duration of the research project. They are fundamental to the research process. Reading and critical engagement with the reading, as well as writing critically and reflectively are common to most forms of research, but dialogue is the kernel of educational action research. Sharing the most tentative of ideas, explaining actions and subjecting your emergent theory to rigorous critique with critical others lies at the heart of the process.

While the focus of educational action research is always on oneself in terms of one's learning about one's practice, it is never in terms of a solitary "I" (Whitehead 2015, p. 246). It is instead an outward-looking "I" that researches *with* and *for* others and that engages in constant dialogue with critical friends. The predominantly solitary activities of reflection and journal writing transform into a rigorous and robust foundation for educational action research when ideas are shared for critique with others through dialogue. The role of critical friends is of the utmost importance here. Perhaps now would be a good time to revisit and critically reflect on Baskerville and Goldblatt (2009). Their definition of what constitutes a critical friend is similar to ours: "We define a critical friend as a capable reflective practitioner (with integrity and passion for teaching and learning) who establishes safe ways of working and negotiates shared understandings to support and challenge a colleague in the deprivatisation of their practice" (2009, p. 206). We authors view the word "negotiates" here as a synonym for "dialogue."

When we engage in dialogue, we hope that our ideas become clearer. Sometimes, a quick-fire round of question and answer is all that is needed to clarify our thinking, whereas on other occasions, the slow-motion of dialogue over email is more helpful (Glenn *et al.* 2017). Very often we grapple with our shared and often misunderstood meanings as we engage in dialogue as part of our research process. Bohm (2004, p. 7) describes dialogue as "a stream of meaning flowing among and through and between us" and, as we engage in research in the classroom, this stream of meaning helps us clarify our ideas, our values and the very purpose of our research. Delong (2020) believes that dialogue is so important in the research process that it is now included as a research method or data collection tool in its own right. She sees dialogue as: "a practical and rigorous research method that, along with other methods such as action-reflection cycles, video-analysis, journals and narrative inquiry, can strengthen the data used for supporting a claim to know" (Delong 2020, p. 72).

As classroom researchers, we use our conversations with critical others to establish the validity of our new ideas, to add to the rigour and transparency of the research. We will explain this further in Chapter 5.

Classroom educational action research for transformation

The transformative nature of action research has been examined by many since the 1940s when Kurt Lewin began looking at the way in which people could take collaborative action to transform their organisations. Lewin (1946) studied the reflexive nature of the action research processes and recognised that they couldn't be separated from the social context in which they were located. Over the years people like Hilary Bradbury, Wilfred Carr, Stephen Kemmis, Jean McNiff and Jack Whitehead, as well as the authors of this book, to name but a few, have all written about the transformative power of engaging in action research.

As educational action researchers, when we reflect critically on what we are doing and examine our motives and intentions, we can come to see, like Bradbury et al. (2019) that action research

> ... builds in potential for transformative action because of the unusual emphasis on the relational and emotional nature of the learners and a willingness to practice more mutually transformative power.
>
> (Bradbury *et al.* 2019, p. 5)

This means that as we undertake an educational action research project, we anticipate that we will not only transform ourselves, our thinking and our practice, but we may also begin a process of working towards a better world. Soon though, we begin to realise that we are doing the research to become better at what we do, because what we do has huge implications for others.

Therefore we each decide what to focus on within our practice; we each reflect critically on the values that inform both our understanding of, and the lived reality of, our practice. When we have clearly identified and articulated those unique and personal professional values, we say, for example, "I can clearly see that I value children's voices in the classroom." Then we can select that particular value as one of the criteria by which we can evaluate the quality of our research. We discuss this in greater detail in Chapter 5. We can claim that we have learned to continue striving to do our best to provide opportunities for children's voices to be heard. We can observe ourselves - and invite others to observe us - in action and check to see if that value is being lived in practice.

We need to be rigorous in our approach to ensure the validity of what we do. The concepts of validity and rigour, along with more explanations and examples of values as the criteria and living standards of judgement, will be developed further in Chapters 4 and 5.

We are choosing a research approach that is grounded in asking critical questions. At the heart of what we do is a wish to live a fulfilled life in a socially just world (Freire 1970;

Roche 2015). Our classrooms are part of a greater community and are inhabited by the citizens of the world in which we live. Like Whitehead (2018, p. 1), we use the term "educational" when it refers to learning that is concerned with both enhancing the realisation of one's own values in practice, and "contributing to the flourishing of humanity, flourishing of my humanity, the humanity of other people, and the flourishing of humanity as a species." As professional educators and researchers, we take this responsibility on board.

When we ask questions about education, we are engaging with ideas that have been long debated by people who practise and write about critical pedagogy. These people include Henry Giroux, Maxine Greene, Peter McLaren, Antonia Darder and many others, all of whom were influenced by the work of Paulo Freire. They all see education as a political act and a process through which people are either oppressed or liberated. They all urge educators to imagine a more just society and to work towards establishing equity and social justice in their educational settings, so as to transform society and the world. These are the same kind of ideas that animate current educational action researchers.

Conclusion

By engaging in educational action research, seeking to improve what we do and deepen our understanding of why we work the way we do, we hope to heighten our own and our students' awareness of social issues and deepen our and their understanding of how we all can become active agents in the world. The research we are engaged in now involves widening our moral imagination and encourages us to be social beings who think independently. We hope that we will maintain our philosophical and intellectual curiosity throughout our professional and personal lives.

Having done this preliminary work on thinking about the broad sweep of values that inform your practice, it is now time to zone in on what may be the potential focus of your study.

In the next chapter you begin the formal planning of your research project.

Additional reading suggestions

Freire, P. (1990) *Pedagogy of the Oppressed*, New York: Continuum. (Chapter 2).
Glenn, M., McDonagh, C., Sullivan, B. and Roche, M. (2017) *Learning Communities in Educational Partnerships: Action Research as Transformation*, London, UK; New York, NY, USA: Bloomsbury Academic (Chapter 1).
Robertson, J. (2000) 'The three Rs of action research methodology: reciprocity, reflexivity and reflection-on-reality', *Educational Action Research*, 8(2), 307–326, available 10.1080/09650790000200124.

Suggested resources

Anastasia Samaras and Mieke Lunenburg: *Introducing Self-Study – a webinar*, (Video) https://youtu.be/oHhGIPM9LFA
Jack Whitehead: *How might people begin to do Living Educational Theory research?* (Video) https://youtu.be/ef4DYIYNONA
Stephen Brookfield: *Keynote at NEARIMeet 17 April 2021* (Video) https://youtu.be/OAtmKEsy1sw?t=165

3 Planning a research project

In this chapter you will be introduced to the practicalities involved in undertaking an educational action research project. There will be a continuing focus on values and on their significance throughout the whole process of researching your practice. You have already been introduced to the concept of reflecting on your values and innermost beliefs in earlier chapters. We will now elaborate on these concepts. We will discuss how to articulate your values and how to determine whether or not you are living to them. These are important considerations and your research topic will evolve from an examination of your beliefs and values as they are enacted in your educational practice. You may also find that, as you carry out your research, your values provide a framework for evaluating the progress of your research.

The chapter is divided into three sections. Section 1 deals with the practical tasks you should undertake at this stage of the research process. In the second section, we will read of how one teacher used her values and her professional reading to formulate her educational action research plan. The final section will outline why values are of the utmost importance in research in practice.

Among the practical elements that we will discuss in this chapter are:

- the importance of values and re-examining them in light of new thinking
- the need for continued, wide-ranging professional reading
- continuing the process of critical reflection and writing in your research journal
- engaging with a critical friend or friends
- data gathering strategies
- ethical issues
- criteria and standards of judgement
- drawing up a research timeline

Section 1: Practical tasks to help plan an educational action research project

You have now reached the stage of beginning to plan your research project. You have established what is important for you in your classroom and you have decided to do something about it. Pause for a moment to take a breath and appreciate the importance of

DOI: 10.4324/9781003288183-4

what you are doing. You are taking responsibility for your professionalism and doing something about it. While new researchers sometimes find that it can be a little daunting to begin to think of oneself now as a researcher or theory generator (McNiff and Whitehead 2006), you will find yourself becoming agentic about your practice and taking charge of your own learning.

There are some tasks that you need to undertake as you prepare your plan. In this section of the chapter, we will explore these tasks and in the process establish your positionality as a beginning practitioner researcher. Some jobs are ongoing and some you will need to do just once. We will outline them here and then discuss how you might engage in them.

Ongoing tasks

As we said earlier, your research is being formulated from the values you hold. Your planning should reflect the fact that you are enquiring into how you might make your practice more commensurate with your values and how you might enhance your practice in that process. Go back to your earlier journal entries and examine what you have said about your values. Do you need to tweak or adapt what you have written? If so, note this and note why. This is a key part of your reflective activity and also your reflexivity, as outlined in Chapter 2.

Awareness of values

Teaching is a value-laden endeavour (Hogan 2011) and educational action research is also value-laden (Whitehead and McNiff 2006). The notion of living to your values should always be about enacting them so as to promote social, ethical and environmental justice. The values that you hold are the foundations that inspire your work and the overarching principles towards which you aspire. Some people find it relatively easy to state their educational values, while others hold their values at a more intuitive level and it takes some time for them to be able to identify and articulate them. For most, the process of doing research into their practice as a teacher is about clarifying their values and seeing where and how these values might be lived in their practice.

Reading

You will probably have engaged in some professional reading at this stage. Remember that you may need to write a *Literature Review* for a written report or dissertation, so we re-iterate the need to keep a record of the authors you have read, including details such as their names, the date of publication, the titles of the books and where you can locate them. Try to read critically and take time to reflect on what you have learned and how it influences your thinking, your values and your practice.

Reflecting critically and writing in your reflective journal

You have read about the importance of critical reflection, and of writing in your journal, in earlier chapters. Be sure to continue this practice because it can become a way of tracking any changes in your thinking, as well as highlighting new learning and new awareness of your values, and can provide insights throughout your research journey.

Talking and sharing ideas

One of the tasks for this stage of your research journey is to talk about your ideas and to share your thinking with others.

Planning tasks

Research planning should be both strong and flexible. Teachers are always adapting their plans in response to the ebb and flow that is normal in every classroom, while keeping a sharp eye to ensure that everything that needs to be done, *is* done. A similar attitude is needed in planning research too, and a clear but flexible approach is needed. Since Covid-19 closures and restrictions impacted all schools in 2020, teachers and teacher researchers have learned, with renewed clarity, the importance of flexibility. It is important to remember that your research is based on the living, everyday practice of your classroom. It will embrace Covid-19 related restrictions as well as any other obstacles that might come your way. You will be able to embed any changes you need to make to your research plan.

Engaging with critical friends

At this stage, your critical friend(s) will need to be able to put some time aside to be able to talk to you and to be able to listen to your ideas as you engage in dialogue with them around your research. They should be able to assist you in testing if your ideas around planning are feasible and if values are being lived in your practice. With their permission, you should make notes during your dialogue session, and you could date these and keep them safely in your data archive. Student teachers usually find that, aside from discussions with tutors, talking to colleagues and establishing a peer-learning network to discuss their research is useful (Brennan 2019).

Here are some simple examples to show what we mean:

Joan, a secondary level teacher, believed in the capability of all to learn. She planned to teach a series of lessons to her pupils. Her research plan was to pre- and post-testing her pupils on the lesson content to show enhancement in her practice. Joan's critical friends pointed out that her research plan was limited in that it was disconnected from her values; gave no voice to her pupils and therefore did not respect them as rational self-determining beings; and it also denied her presence in the research process.

Paul worked with 12-year-old pupils. Many of them did not have English as a first language and all came from what was designated as a disadvantaged environment. He planned not to send permission notes for the research to their parents as it was unlikely that they would be returned, so he had another teacher co-sign them with the students. He felt that it was adequate for a responsible and literate adult to co-sign the permission notes. Paul's critical friends argued that his plan undermined the ethics and integrity of the research process.

Deciding on a research question

You have now spent some time reflecting critically on your area of concern or interest and exploring why you are concerned or interested. Your research question may change over time, but it is important to begin to establish one now. As action researchers usually ask questions like "How might I enhance my practice?", you will probably have an "I" in your research question. This is because your research is about you and your practice – along with others, such as your pupils, your colleagues or pupils' parents, perhaps. Your research question might be something like "How might I enhance my teaching of multiplication tables so that everyone in my class can access the maths curriculum with ease?" or "How might I create an environment in my classroom where everyone speaks in a mutually respectful manner?" The range of areas to research is as broad, unique and diverse as the values you hold, and the way you choose to show how you might live them in your practice will be unique also. Two researchers might have the same question but their research process will be as unique as themselves.

Thinking about data

Now is a good time to think about the type of data you might like to collect. We will discuss data in greater detail in Chapters 4 and 5, but for now, it is a good idea to plan how you might do this. If you are exploring how you might live more closely to your value of inclusion, as you teach reading, for example, then much of the data will be collected during a reading lesson. The data might be in the form of voice recordings or extracts of conversations with your pupils. However, you might also keep a close eye on how you see your values being enacted in your practice in other class periods, or during playtime. You might spot pupils reading a book together, with one helping the other, during a break time, and this too could be useful data to show how your values are being enacted in your practice. A colleague might tell you informally in the staffroom that they noticed children reading books in the corridor waiting outside classrooms. A lot of data can be happenstance or chance, like this. You need to be alert and open to it. Collecting samples of children's work or having conversations with pupils' parents could also be strategies that would help your research.

It would be a good idea to make a list of possible data collection strategies and tools. Some examples might be transcripts of conversations with pupils, colleagues, parents and critical friends; observations made during class; excerpts from letters and emails; voice recordings or video clips or photographs (if allowed); questionnaires; interviews; artefacts from the classroom or samples of pupils' work. Some teachers like to collect test scores to help outline and track how their practice is improving and how their practice is becoming more commensurate with their values or with curricula values. It might be worth considering if there are value tensions, as discussed in Chapter 2, here or not.

One of the richest sources of data will undoubtedly be your reflective journal. Here you will be able to track any new insights you have discovered and any new learning that you have encountered. You will also be able to explain your own reactions over time to your research project. Your journal will contain the account of how you have tried to enhance your practice, your responses to the process, how you are becoming more aware of your values and how you have tested your values, to see if they are being lived in your practice.

Ethical permission

Gaining ethical permission to undertake research with your pupils, or your colleagues, is of crucial importance. If you are undertaking research in a formal programme, then the programme providers will usually have a set of ethical procedures that you need to follow and probably copies of sample letters to be sent to governing boards, school principals or headteachers, pupils, colleagues and parents or guardians. It is important to remember that your research process should respect the rights of all participants, that it should cause no harm to either participants or yourself as researcher, and that it requires the active, informed consent of all. If you need more guidance on ethical approval, the *Ethical Guidelines for Educational Research*, published by the British Educational Research Association (BERA, 2018) is a useful guide. It is expected that you bring your own integrity and ethical values to the planning of the research project as well as following the guidelines provided. We will discuss ethics in educational action research in greater detail in Chapter 4.

Generate some criteria or standards of judgement

Researchers who are involved in quality research in their practice will want to demonstrate their rigour. You can do so by following Habermas's (1976) guidelines around speaking comprehensibly, with authenticity, and in a truthful and appropriate manner. You may also seek critique and validation from others, from the outset of the research, so as to avoid the pitfalls of becoming too introspective.

You can establish criteria and standards of judgement (Whitehead and McNiff 2006) by which you can ascertain if, in fact, you are working more closely to your values and enhancing your practice. Take for example Peter's action research project. He wanted to explore how he might enhance his teaching of well-being to 14-year-olds as he sought to express his values of care and compassion more fully in his practice. He established that (i) if he heard or saw his students express contentment with their lives and (ii) if he heard or saw his students trying to connect and be aware of one another's concerns, these could be criteria by which he could judge the quality of his research. These criteria were indicators or signs that showed that he was doing what he said he was doing. We will explore this idea in greater detail in Chapter 5.

Draw up a timeline

Your timeline should be do-able. You should try to slot it into your usual schedule so that it nearly becomes a natural add-on to your everyday life. While it should give a structure to your research project in terms of timings, you should be ready to adjust it, if something unexpected arises. A sample timeline for a year-long project for academic accreditation might look something like Figure 3.1:

July - September	Think about what is important about your work, the values you hold and your identity as an educator. Begin to write a reflective journal and do some professional reading
October - January	Think about, and refine your research question Seek and receive ethical permission from all necessary bodies (schools, university, pupils, parents, colleagues etc.) Prepare for data collection Continue your reflective journal and professional reading. Discuss thinking with critical friends Begin draft writing of elements of the research report or dissertation (draft literature review, draft methodology section or perhaps a background to your research)
February – May	Begin your research project or intervention Consider the criteria by which you might evaluate the quality of your work Collect data Reflect on process, examine and analyse data. Continue your journal, professional reading and draft writing. Discuss thinking with critical friendsCollect data
May - June	Complete the project work, data collection. Reflect on process, examine and analyse data. Continue journaling, reading and discussing your ideas with critical friends and your validation group. Begin formal writing elements of the report.
July	Complete data analysis and establish areas of new learning in terms of linking tvalues to practice Consider the significance of the work in terms of your educational influence in your own learning, in the learning of others and in the policy of the organisation in which you work. Continue reading, reflecting and discussing your thinking with critical friends/validation group Complete the first draft of the research report and submit it to your supervisor, if working on an accredited programme, or to another reader if not.
August - October	Redraft and complete final draft of report Share learning with others informally
November	Share your research with the wider public via written report or journal article, presentation, web-based contribution – webinar or blog.

Figure 3.1 A sample timeline for a year-long project for academic accreditation

Writing tasks

By now you have had an opportunity to become comfortable with your journal writing and you will see how some of your practice writing might become part of a written report. Try to use your writing to help you articulate your values and your critical reflection. It is also a good idea to use your drafting and redrafting of your ideas to help you fine-tune the focus of your research and ensure that it is a manageable project.

Now try these writing exercises:

My research question is …
I want to find out more about… .because … or
I am concerned about … because …
My values of … animate my life. I can see these values being enacted when …

Draw up a research plan that would be manageable in your classroom situation and within your timeframe.

We have synopsised the tasks outlined above in Figure 3.2:

Ongoing tasks	Yes	No	Under way
Reflecting on and clarifying values	—	—	—
Broaden your reading. Include policy and practices issues, as well as the values and concepts that influence them.	—	—	—
Writing a reflective journal and re-reading it	—	—	—
Talking and sharing your ideas	—	—	—

Planning tasks	Yes	No	Under way
Find some critical friends	—	—	—
Imagine possibilities in response to your concerns and decide on a plan of action	—	—	—
Check the plan is manageable within the given time frame. Check that the plan is flexible in case of interruptions to the implementation of your plan.	—	—	—
Decide on a possible research question and course of action for enhancing your practice	—	—	—
Think about data	—	—	—
Get ethical permission	—	—	—
Generate some criteria	—	—	—

Writing Tasks	Yes	No	Under way
Have you experienced yourself as a 'living contradiction' (Whitehead 1989)?	—	—	—
Write a research question	—	—	—
Make a research plan and draw up a timeline (as part of a draft methodology section of a report)	—	—	—

Figure 3.2 Tasks to help you plan your research project

Section 2: A teacher's account of how her professional reading and her values influenced her research plan

The following is part of the research account of Norma (pseudonym), a teacher whose role is to support pupils from a minority group at primary school level. Her story is about how she came to understand the quality of education offered and what this looked like within the schooling system. In the following extracts from her research, she explains how her onto-logical values provided her with her research topic, and how her professional reading in-fluenced her research plan. She recounts how her values permeated her research and how they underpinned the standards of judgement for assessing the research.

Social justice and equality are two of my ontological values, and as such they form the living standards by which I judge the quality of my work. Principles of social justice and equality were in fact the impetus that inspired me to undertake my research. My research account is the narrative of my investigation into how, in the interest of social justice, the opportunities that are currently available to the majority of children in the educational system, could also be extended to children from minority groups. The process of engaging in this investigation has enabled me to generate a theory of my living educational practice as a site for the promotion of social justice through the practice of inclusion, and as equality of respect for all pupils. Principles of social justice and equality are intrinsic to my account of my research for the following reasons:

1   they serve as the core values underpinning my research, and informing my ontological commitments to living a life grounded in these values
2   they constitute the frameworks within which my research is located
3   they provide the basis for the articulation and validation of my claims to knowledge, which emerge from my living educational practice

For Norma, the answer to the question "What is my concern?" was that she wished to see all children benefitting equally from the education system. Her answer to the question "Why am I concerned?" was that she wanted to fulfil her commitment to her values. You can see then that Norma's research topic was firmly rooted in her values of social justice and equity. As she continues to formulate her research plan, she describes her understanding of social justice, which became an overarching framework for her research. She compares the dis-tributive concept of social justice, as found in the literature, with her lived experience of the practice of social justice.

I propose, therefore, to explain the relevance to my research of issues of social justice and equality, both at the theoretical level, in relation to the theories in the literature, and at the level of practice, in relation to living theories that emerged from my practice as the lived reality of social justice and equality.

There are many factors that can contribute to situations of injustice and inequality. For example, people can be born into different social groups, resulting in those born into a higher socio-economic group having greater financial advantages than those born into a lower socio-economic group. This inequality can have major repercussions in that it can persist throughout life and can permeate all areas of existence, where goods and services can be bought by those with the capacity to pay for them, thus adding to the privileges enjoyed by those from the higher socio-economic groups. In this context, Rawls' (1971) theory of the distributive paradigm of social justice is relevant. Rawls (1971, p. 4) states that the principles of social justice "provide a way of assigning rights and duties in the basic institutions of society and they define the appropriate distribution of the benefits and burdens of social cooperation."

However, while it may be appropriate to consider the division of material social goods within a distributive framework of social justice, the concept of justice itself does not appear to fit into the category of goods that can be shared out in numerical fashion. Justice can be perceived as a quality in relationships that can lead to just practices. Young (1990, p. 8) suggests that "contemporary philosophical theories of justice tend to restrict the meaning of social justice to the morally proper distribution of benefits and burdens among society's members."

She argues that, instead, the focus should be on concepts of domination and oppression, which are at the root of injustice. In agreement with Young (1990), therefore, I suggest that, in accordance with principles of social justice, we need to challenge current practices of institutionalised domination and oppression.

From the above discussion, you can see the importance of continuous reflection throughout your research and the significance of critical engagement with the literature as you develop and carry out your research plan. If Norma had accepted unthinkingly some of the ideas on social justice that she encountered initially in the literature, she would have been influenced by a rather restrictive portrayal of social justice as a quantity to be divided equally among all recipients. Further reading, coupled with her own reflections, led her to a more life-affirming concept of justice as the assignment of resources to each according to their needs. However, this does not easily translate into practice, as the following extract indicates.

In theory, it should be possible to ensure that social justice acts as a guiding principle in the provision of educational services, provided that all involved in the provision are in agreement that this is the best way of achieving fairness and equality for those at the receiving end. In accordance with the Education Act (Government of Ireland 1998) education is available to all, not on an invitational basis but as a compulsory regime for all children between the ages of six and sixteen. One would expect, then, that all children would be treated equally within the educational system. However, this is not always the reality. While all children have equal access to educational provision at primary school level, as required by the Education Welfare Act (Government of Ireland 2000),

> very often the equality ends here. Many schools seem to think that, in accepting all applicants, they are demonstrating non-discriminatory practices, and that this fulfils their obligation to treat all children equally. They do not, therefore, perceive the need for continuity of the concept of equality, to ensure that it extends to equality of participation, opportunity or outcome.

In engaging with the literature, Norma had accessed an educational policy that seemed to guarantee equity for all children within the education system. However, as she reflected critically on her reading, she realised that the equity only extended to equality of access. The policy ensured that all children had access to schooling but did not grant them equal entitlement in terms of the resources they would need in order to achieve equality of participation, achievement or outcome. Norma was beginning to realise that there can often be a chasmic gap between policy and practice. However, she encountered the views of one educationalist that gave her hope for a more equitable provision of education for all children.

> One educationalist, who supports the idea of a living system of education so that every child can learn and achieve, is Zappone (2002), who recommends a framework that includes a description of the process and overall objective of achieving equality in children's educational provision. She emphasises that she is describing a process, rather than a static reality, which would involve educationalists in the dynamism of substantive change. Zappone (2002, p. 82) suggests that "achieving equality in children's education requires a living system that:
>
> - Supports common ways of learning
> - Accommodates diverse capacities, cultures, learning paths and achievement outcome
> - Enables communal solidarity or 'sticking together'
> - Reduces inequalities of resources between social groups and geographical communities."

Influenced by these ideas, Norma came to the conclusion that her educational practice should represent the living realisation of the principles to which she was committed, in order to achieve a more equitable educational provision for all children. She realised that the ideals contained in policy documents needed to be evident in her practice if she were to achieve her aim of developing an inclusive practice based on diversity, solidarity and shared experiences. Norma's claim that she succeeded in living to her values in her educational practice is described briefly in the following extract:

> I contend that, through the transformation of the concept of equality into lived reality in my practice, I have moved beyond a strictly propositional form of theory to engage in a living form of theory. Through presenting an account of my practice, I demonstrate

> how I have transformed that practice into a more socially just one, by living in the direction of my ontological values of justice and entitlement. The significance of my work, therefore, can be judged in terms of its contribution to new practices that reflect principles of social justice and equality, and also in terms of its contribution to new forms of theory that can be shown as the living out of the values that inform my work.

The extract from Norma's research as outlined above will have given you an idea of the importance of deep reflection on your values and of how this can influence your research plan. It will have indicated to you how your values can provide the rationale for your research question as well as the conceptual frameworks within which you can locate your research as you engage in the research process. You should now have a clearer picture of how your values can be used for the purpose of assessing your research and for articulating the significance of your research. You can see also how the various threads that make up a research plan can be woven together through critical engagement with the literature: your values, your research topic, critical reflection, your rationale for undertaking your research and the standards of judgement for evaluating your research, all contribute to creating the rich tapestry of your research plan.

Section 3: Looking at values from a theoretical perspective

In this section we look at

- why values are important in planning your research
- types of values
- the process of articulating your values

In earlier chapters we looked at the idea of living contradiction i.e when our practice is not as we would like it to be. This leads to asking why we would like it to be that way, in other words to a critical examination of our values and how they are or are not lived in our practice.

Personal and professional values, though often eschewed in traditional forms of research, form the foundations of many approaches to educational action research. They are the deeply held beliefs we hold that inform our integrity and identity as we work towards a good and more socially just world. They are the underpinning principles and overarching guidelines that guide our lives. The enactment of one's values can pose problems in itself because (i) not everyone holds the same values and (ii) the question of what we mean by "good" is open to interpretation. These ideas are examined well in Wood (2014, p. 37) who "problematises the notion that 'good' values lead to 'good' action." It is important to be aware that our understanding of our values becomes clearer as they emerge in the research process.

Given the busy nature of our professional lives as teachers, our values may not always be to the forefront of our minds. If you have not formed the habit of reflecting on your educational practice, you may not have had the opportunity to articulate your values or to state them explicitly. Therefore, it may require a nudge or a prompt to be able to name them and bring them into focus so that you may reflect on them.

How do you begin the process of articulating your values? You could start by examining what is meant by "values." Johnson (2012) provides a succinct explanation of the term "value" when he suggests that a value can be anything that we find to be of importance or of worth. One strategy, therefore, that could help you to identify your values, is to ask questions such as "What is important to me as a teacher? As a teacher, what do I hope to achieve?" See McDonagh *et al.* (2020, pp. 34–37) for more questions like these. When you have es-tablished what it is that you value in terms of your educational life, or what it is that you hope to achieve in your teaching practice, you can identify what matters most to you as a teacher. You can then name these concepts as the values that govern your professional life and according to which you can evaluate your practice.

When you have developed an awareness of your values to the extent that you are quite familiar with them, you can begin to examine them in detail, in terms of how well you are living to your values in your practice and whether or not they are for the "flourishing of humanity" (Whitehead 2018). You will then be well-positioned to gauge the implications for your practice of engaging in critical reflection on your values. It might be a good idea now, to schedule a meeting with your critical friend(s) where you can present your current thinking about your values.

In this context, you can see how your values give meaning and purpose to your life as a teacher.

Why are values important in planning your research?

The significance of naming your values lies in the fact that often this process can provide a starting point for beginning to research your practice in order to enhance it. As you formulate your plan of action, a focus on your values will help you to decide what your concern is and why you are concerned. The idea of a value being an impetus to action is suggested by Storey and Beeman (2009) in their definition of it as an enduring belief about the desirability of some means or action. One of the purposes in naming your values is so that you can aim to live to those values in your teaching life. However, through reflecting critically on your practice, you may discover that you are not actually living to your values. You may, therefore, experience yourself as a living contradiction, as described by Whitehead (2018). This occurs when, on the one hand, you believe that you are living to your expressed values, but the lived reality of your practice does not bear witness to this, resulting in a state of conflict. This realisation of what is occurring in your practice, and the desire to resolve the issue, may help you plan your research. It will also help to identify an area of practice that you can begin to reflect on as you strive to enhance or improve it. These are all essential elements in the planning process.

Types of values

You may find it useful to think about the types of values people may hold. They may be grouped in various ways, depending on the context in which they occur or the circumstances to which they relate. Some people prefer to think about their values in a free, non-categorised manner, while others like to chunk ideas around values into categories as out-lined here. In Chapter 2, we referred to ontological and epistemological values. Other ca-tegories of values that may be of interest to you are professional, personal and educational values. Many institutions and organisations include a set of values in their operational guidelines and mission statements. Ostensibly, members and employees are expected to act according to these values in their practice. In reality, the statement of values may be just a box-ticking exercise, included in documents or laminated and affixed to notice boards be-cause of a requirement to do so, but seldom referred to thereafter. Perhaps those who are expected to commit to the stated values have no sense of ownership of the process. The values may have been thrust upon them, with no input on their part, and so they feel no compunction in regard to living to the values. It is important, therefore, to identify your own values for yourself so that you will feel a commitment to them and see them as living entities in your life, and then, if you wish, align them to other professional values that have been mandated. The Teaching Council of Ireland (2016a) has named four core values of care, respect, integrity and trust that should underpin teachers' professional relationships. We agree that these values are important for teachers.

Ontological values

If you are reflecting on how you relate to other people, and in particular looking at the quality of the relationship, you may want those relationships to be respectful of others and caring towards them. In relation to your friends, you might feel that it is important to have a sense of trust between you. You can then name your values as respect, care and trust. Because these values relate to your way of being with others, you could call them your ontological values, based on an interpretation of ontology as your way of being in the world and your relationships with others whom you encounter in your world.

Epistemological values

When you think about knowledge, how it is created and who can create it, you are establishing your epistemological stance in life. Views on knowledge can vary, depending on whether you view it as something fixed that can be transferred to others by those in possession of the knowledge, or whether you see it as something that is constantly evolving and changing while being created in your interactions with others. For example, do you see yourself as the person owning the knowledge and imparting it to your students? This model of knowledge trans-mission is described by Rogers and Freiberg (1994) in the metaphor of the jug, for example, the teacher, filling the empty mug, i.e. the student, with ready-made information to be assimilated unthinkingly. Freire (1972) is equally scathing of such a scenario, which he calls the banking system, where the teacher gives the information to the student to be stored in the student's memory until required to be reproduced in an examination, thus depriving the student of any sense of agency or ownership of the knowledge. More recently, we see the notion of teachers as mere "deliverers of content" and "knowledge brokers" (Goodwin 2021, p. 15) re-emerging. Is your interpretation of knowledge acquisition represented by the passive approach as described by the authors above, or do you see knowledge as co-created in the interactions between you and your students? If the latter represents your view of knowledge, you can say that knowledge creation is one of your epistemological values.

Professional values

You can have values that are related to the things that you regard as important in a teaching and learning situation, and which appear to have particular significance in your professional life as an educator. If you are committed to working closely with your colleagues, then perhaps you can claim to value cooperation, collaboration and collegiality. You may regard equity as an important quality in your relationships with colleagues if you wish to avoid the formation of a hierarchical system that could lead to the disempowerment or exclusion of some voices. Inclusion may also be a feature of your interactions with colleagues if you wish to see all having the opportunity of participating in dialogue and professional conversations so that no one feels excluded, or marginalised, or not valued.

Personal values

Your personal life may be governed by certain values to which you feel a strong commitment. Gamage *et al.* (2021) suggest that such values can contribute to the building of one's personal and social identity. These values may be deeply-embedded traits to which you feel a sense of loyalty. Personal values might include love, respect, care and trust. These values relate to how you live your life and how you interact with others. They are, therefore, similar to ontological values and may also overlap with your professional values. Overlap between sets of values is perfectly natural, as is the prioritisation of some values over others at various stages of your life.

Educational values

Educational values are frequently mentioned in discussions about what matters in education. They refer to your actions in the classroom and to your relationships with students. For example, you may wish to see your students become independent learners and consequently encourage them to take responsibility for their own learning. If you believe that students can contribute in a meaningful way to the teaching and learning in your classroom, you might value a social constructivist approach to pedagogy. Values around independent learning and social constructivism could be described as educational values.

What we have outlined here are some of the kinds of values to which you, as an educator, can relate but there may well be other categories which are pertinent also. As mentioned above, these groupings are not fixed and there is often a crossover between the various groups of values. Some values may be relevant in more than one context. You may therefore be flexible in your understanding of your values and adopt a broad conceptualisation of how they can relate to the various areas of your life and research.

The process of articulating your values

As you plan your research project, you will realise that the values you hold lie at the heart of the research. Sometimes the identification, clarification and articulation of one's values can be a slow process. Often they only begin to emerge in the process of the research, as you reflect critically on your practice and become involved in a process of coming to know yourself as a person and as a professional. For some, the articulation of one's values becomes the focus of the research itself (Glenn 2006). A teacher's identity and integrity are fundamental to good teaching according to Palmer (2017), and Kelchtermans (2009) similarly argues that the person of the teacher is a vital element in professional teaching. The process of coming to know oneself is not automatic and takes some time and involves a good deal of reflection. Palmer suggests that teachers need not only to reflect but also to talk to one another about their "inner lives" and "who they are as teachers" (2017, p. 12). As educational action researchers, we link identity and integrity to our innermost values and beliefs. We acknowledge therefore that our values gradually emerge and become clearer in the research process (Whitehead 2018).

Living contradiction

As we mentioned in the introduction, there may be occasions where you find that you are not living to the values that you profess to hold. You may be under the misapprehension, initially, that you are actually living to your values and may only discover that this is not the case through your reflection on your practice, or from the feedback that you get from colleagues or critical friends. This phenomenon has been described by Whitehead (2018) as experiencing oneself as a living contradiction. It is a position in which you will not feel comfortable if you have a sincere wish to be true to your stated values. Kelchtermans calls this a "discomforting experience" (2009, p. 270). Therefore, it is not a situation that you can contemplate as continuing indefinitely and so you may feel compelled to resolve the cause of the conflict in an expeditious manner and in a way that will enable you to experience the reality of living to your values.

It takes courage to acknowledge that you are not living to your values and to come to a decision to do something about the issue. However, such perspicacity can be beneficial in a number of ways. You may be spurred to take action aimed at reversing the situation and thus find yourself beginning the process of trying to live more closely to your values. You could be inspired to adopt a more critical approach to your reflection on your practice. As a result, you may develop a more heightened awareness around your values and about how they are enacted in your practice. You would then be better positioned to know when your actions are not commensurate with your values, and could begin to move forward by developing a plan to bring about a greater alignment between your values and your actions.

Sometimes, the denial of your values in your practice may be caused by you or your actions, in which case you may feel that the responsibility for resolving the situation lies with you. You may find it relatively easy to resolve the issue and restore your practice to one that evidences your values. Conversely, there are some issues that arise from within us that despite our best efforts, are difficult to control or resolve. For example, you may feel you value kindness and patience in your teaching but yet, you find that irritation and bad temper feature strongly in your everyday practice. This would be a very serious issue for any teacher and should demand immediate action, up to and including leaving the profession entirely. While some internally sourced tensions can be easily resolved, others can prove very difficult.

There may also be occasions where the denial of your values stems from external sources, outside of your control. Such instances may be more difficult, if not impossible, to resolve, as the circumstances are beyond your control. For example, your value of inclusion could be reflected in your wish to integrate fully into your classroom, students with special educational needs. Your school, on the other hand, may pursue a policy of withdrawing such students regularly for resource teaching, making it difficult for you to live to your value of inclusion as fully as you would like. There may be no easy solution to this conflict and you may have to try to live with it, perhaps by finding creative and innovative ways to ensure that the students experience inclusion at every possible opportunity. Sometimes, values that contradict our sense of justice, or that are a discriminatory feature in our workplaces, may be direct examples of the practice of hegemony that exists in many systems (see Chapter 2).

Imagining

Planning your research is also about using your imagination to visualise what a better version of your practice and your world might be like. Tapping into your creative intentions and trusting your own energy, instincts and constellation of values helps you to see beyond what currently exists as you envision new pathways and possibilities (O'Donohue 2003). Taking time out to reflect, read and talk to others can both ignite our imaginations as well as illuminate the practical constraints of our imagined plans.

Conclusion

From your engagement with the ideas and activities in this chapter, you will now have an awareness of the importance of values to the process of planning and undertaking educational action research in your practice. You have been introduced to the various elements involved in drawing up your research plan: choosing a research question, critically engaging with relevant literature, writing regularly in your research journal, engaging with a critical friend, ethical considerations and data collection. You should also have a clearer understanding of the necessity to constantly reflect on your values to ascertain whether or not you are living to them as you carry out your research. Your reflective journal, documenting the course of your research, and your reflections on it, now becomes part of your daily routine and will inform your research plan. It will form a significant part of the data that you will need in order to provide evidence of your learning as a result of engaging in your research. In the next chapter, we will look at various methods of data collection that are suitable for practitioners researching their own educational practice.

Additional reading suggestions

Bruce Ferguson, P. (2015) 'Who am I who teaches?', *Educational Journal of Living Theories*, 8(1), 49–66, available: https://www.ejolts.net/files/Bruce_Ferguson8%281%29.pdf. (Open Access)

Kelchtermans, G. (2009) 'Who I am in how I teach is the message: self-understanding, vulnerability and reflection', *Teacher and Teaching: Theory and Practice*, 15(2), 257–272, available: 10.1080/1354 0600902875332.

Palmer, P. (n.d.) *The Heart of a Teacher: Identity and Integrity in Teaching*, available: https://couragerenewal.org/library/the-heart-of-a-teacher/ [accessed 2 September 2022] (Open Access)

Suggested resources

Whitehead, J. (2022) *'Values in Living Educational Theory'*, *Jack Whitehead in Conversation*, [video], available: https://youtu.be/oeugtwatmjA, [accessed 27 January 2023].

Whitehead, J. (n.d.) *How do I Improve What I Am Doing? Action-Reflection Planner for Improving Learning and Generating a Living-Educational-Theory*, available: https://www.actionresearch.net/writings/jack/arlivingtheoryplanner.pdf., [accessed 7 August 2022].

4 Collecting and using data

In this chapter you will have the opportunity to engage with all aspects of data collection. It is important to remember throughout, that your research is being carried out on yourself and on your practice. This focus should be reflected in how and where you collect your data. Teacher researchers collect data to help them describe and explain to others what is happening in their practice. Unless they are invited in physically to observe the teacher, these others can only see into the researchers' classrooms by hearing, seeing or reading the researchers' written accounts of their research. The researchers also seek data to show changes in their thinking. Finally, they mine their data for examples of enhanced practice, new insights into practice and links between their values and their practice.

Section 1 of this chapter will serve as a guide through the practical aspects of preparation for data collection. In Section 2 you will be given an example of how a teacher undertaking research in her practice gathered data. Section 3 explores why data collection is important and the various approaches used in gathering data.

Section 1: Practical preparation: Looking at and describing the situation as it is right now and during your research

In this section you will encounter:

- defining data
- initial data collection to show the situation as it was prior to your research
- choosing data collection tools
- collecting your data
- triangulation of your data
- ethical issues
- attitude towards participants
- making effective use of your data

We begin by asking "what is data?" Data is a scholarly word for information and its purpose is to tell you more about a situation. We collect data to allow others to see into our classrooms and to show how our practice changes as we research it. Teachers are constantly collecting data about their teaching in their classroom settings, through conversations with their students, observing actions and interactions, noting student and staff attendance, as

DOI: 10.4324/9781003288183-5

well as through exam results, standardised and teacher-designed testing. Assessment data is used to inform planning for teaching and learning. Education students use the data they gather on placement to inform their daily or weekly reflections. Research data, "unlike other types of information, is collected, observed, or created, for the purpose of validating research findings" (University of Leeds 2022, np) and to produce original research results. Later we will discuss the most relevant ways of collecting data to suit your research focus. For now, we begin with the initial data collection process.

Initial data collection

Data collection is an important aspect of your research and needs to be undertaken in a stringent and rigorous manner. By rigorous, we mean that the data collected should be accurate, credible and honestly reflect the situation in your practice.

Initially, data is gathered to show the situation as it was prior to your research. You could aim to gather some data before you begin your research so that you can show what the situation was prior to carrying out your action plan.

This is where your research journal will play an important role as you reflect on and explain the situation at the outset. You will then be able to demonstrate whether or not the situation has improved or changed in any way as a result of undertaking your research. Gathering such data could also provide you with a rationale for your choice of research topic. This can occur as you reflect on your practice, describe the situation that existed before you began your research and explain why you wished to undertake this particular piece of research. To ensure the rigour of your data collection, it would be a good idea to keep a written record of it in your research journal. You will then have a reference point when you will be required to provide evidence of change or enhancement in your practice.

If you are wondering what exactly you should keep notes on, Hughes and William (2001) recommend the following format for your note-taking:

> What you observe (see or hear),
> What happens, and what happens next,
> What you think, guess, wonder about, or conclude,
> What you feel,
> What you plan or dream.

Hughes and William (2001, np)

They suggest keeping these notes under different headings or descriptions so that you can differentiate between what you actually saw, what you were told about and what you planned or dreamed. Whatever system you decide to use for documenting your data, you will need to ensure that it is methodical and rigorous, and that it will stand up to scrutiny.

Data collection tools

Consider choosing data collection tools that are commensurate with your values and with an educational action research methodology. Data collection tools refer to the methods, devices and instruments researchers use to collect data. The data collection tools that you choose will depend on the type of data you wish to gather. Data can be either quantitative or qualitative. Quantitative data, as discussed in Chapter 1, refers to data that can be measured, that can be verified numerically or that can be scientifically proven. Generally, it would be heavily reliant on numerical and statistical findings. Traditional researchers, using a positivist approach to research, tend to rely almost exclusively on quantitative means of data collection, because they believe it guarantees certainty, accuracy and reliability in their research findings. In an educational action research approach, where the focus is very much on the "I" in terms of the researcher's professional learning and enhancement of practice, and where different epistemological values prevail, the emphasis is more on qualitative means of data collection. Clark *et al.* (2020) suggest that the aim of qualitative data collection is to build a complex and nuanced description of the situation from multiple perspectives.

To ensure that multiple perspectives are represented, qualitative data takes into consideration the opinions of the researcher and other participants in the research. This can be done through the use of questionnaires, conversations, interviews or focus groups. Your research journal is a valuable source of qualitative data and this is why we stress the importance of using it on a daily basis to note your actions and reflections. Educational researchers sometimes use quantitative means of data collection, for example, standardised test scores or results of teacher-designed tests, as they find these easy to acquire and they feel that they can more easily meet the criteria for certainty and accuracy. However, qualitative methods remain the main source of data collection in action research approaches.

As educational action researchers, we collect data to help us outline and track how our practice is improving and how it is becoming more commensurate with our values – or not. We use a variety of data-collecting tools. Along with our reflective journal, these could include transcripts of conversations with pupils, colleagues, parents and critical friends; observations made during class; excerpts from letters and emails; voice recordings (or video clips if allowed, under ethical considerations) of conversations; photographs; artefacts and samples of pupils' work. Teachers may also collect test scores, do questionnaires and conduct interviews.

Critical feedback from participants in the research also plays a significant role in your data collection as it helps verify the honesty of your data. This could include critique from your students, colleagues, critical friends and validation group, as they question your data and your new learning and assess the accuracy of your account. As outlined previously, a critical friend is someone who agrees to become involved in your research from the beginning and to give critical feedback at various stages during the research process. Costa and Kallick (1993, p. 50) describe a critical friend as a "trusted person who asks provocative questions, provides data to be examined through another lens, and offers critique of a person's work as a friend." A similar view of the role of a critical friend as someone who "assists through questioning, reflecting back and providing another viewpoint, promoting honest reflection and reappraisal, a seeing anew that may be challenging and uncomfortable, yet enhancing" is propounded by Swaffield (2008, p. 323).

A validation group consists of professional colleagues and friends, possibly including your critical friend(s), to whom you can present your research so that they may provide validation of your research claim. Whitehead and McNiff (2006, p. 103) suggest that the responsibilities of a validation group are to "listen carefully, to assess the quality of the claim to knowledge in relation to the evidence produced" and to "agree or disagree that the work demonstrates sufficient merit to go forward to the next stages." In Chapter 5 we will look at validation groups in more detail.

Collecting your data

At the outset of your research, you will be required to draw up an action plan, which will include details of your data collection tools. In your research plan, you need to describe the actions you propose taking in order to collect data, as well as the timeframe for completing the actions, as outlined in Chapter 3. Students on teaching placement may be limited in the time available for conducting their research, but they can still find a range of data collection tools. These may include teaching notes; observations; reflections on lessons; comments made by cooperating teachers, tutors and examiners who observe the teaching; artefacts generated during lessons to show how learning is happening, as well as pupils' reactions and comments.

In order to maintain a rigorous approach to your research each piece of data should be dated, signed by the researcher and, if appropriate, signed by those supplying the data. The artefacts and data are then stored in a data archive. This archive may be as simple as a large storage box, or it could be a password-protected virtual folder. We will mention this again in the ethics section of the chapter.

During this phase of your research, constant reflection on your actions will help to ensure rigour in your data collection. Your critical reflections, noted in your reflective journal, will indicate whether or not your research project is having the desired effect on your practice and if you are living more closely to your values. If it is not having the effect you had hoped for, you can record your dissatisfaction with the plan and reflect on why this may be happening. You may then alter your plan and change your data collection tools, if necessary, thus beginning a second research cycle. Your reflections will also show you whether or not you are living to your values and, if you find evidence to indicate that you are not, this is important too. You can query why this is the case and see what you can learn in the process. Very often, these occasions of perceived "failure" can provide the teacher researchers with the richest opportunities for new learning as they grapple with what happened in their research project, and why it happened. If needed, you can review your planned data collection methods and make any necessary changes to ensure that there is alignment between the research process and your values. Re-evaluating your research aims and adjusting your research plans accordingly form an important part of your learning process and will contribute to the creation of new knowledge about your practice. Changes can also come about in other ways, for example, following a discussion with a critical friend or colleague who might see something that you have missed.

Triangulation of your data

Triangulation is a feature of qualitative research, and it is about planning to collect your data in a methodical and rigorous manner. It helps to strengthen the accuracy of your data collection because it requires collecting data from more than two sources. This is relatively easy to accomplish, particularly if you keep this in mind as you plan your data collection tools. We have mentioned, above, several possible data sources. If you use three of these, for example your reflective journal, questionnaires completed by your students and feedback from critical friends, you will be able to triangulate your data. You will then have different perspectives on your research, as well as a variety of interpretations of the outcomes of the research. This will contribute to adding rigour, authenticity and validation to your research findings. It adds to the trustworthiness of your research and can help eliminate the charge of bias, which could result from relying only on your own interpretation of the data.

You will not be relying solely on your own views and conclusions but will have reliable corroboration of your interpretations. According to Cohen *et al.* (2018), triangulation can explain more fully the richness and complexity of what you describe because it is studied from more than one standpoint and therefore can provide a more balanced picture of your research.

Ethical issues

As a teacher researcher you want to ensure that your data collection meets the highest ethical standards. There are a number of ethical issues that need to be addressed prior to undertaking your research. It is generally expected that, when you undertake research in the classroom, everyone involved is aware that you are doing research and therefore gathering data. You should gain ethical approval from all participants (and/or their parents and guardians) who are going to be part of your research.

If you are on an academic programme, you may need to gain ethical approval from the college or university where you are undertaking your studies. For this purpose, you will need to submit a brief summary of your research plan, including details of your participants and your data collection instruments. When you have obtained ethical approval, you will then need to seek permission from the institution and individuals directly involved in the research. You will need permission from your school principal/headteacher or Board of Management/Governing Body in order to carry out your research in your classroom and you should provide them with a brief summary of your proposed action plan.

If you are a student teacher, such permissions are equally important. You will need to establish, by checking with your teacher education programme provider and with your co-operating school, what the required ethical guidelines are. Once you are clear on these guidelines, it is expected that you should adhere strictly to them.

Your students, who will be participating in your research, will be required to give their assent and so it is important that they understand clearly what is involved in opting to participate. They would need, therefore, to have the research project explained to them in a manner suited to their age and level of understanding. If the students are minors, permission for their participation should be sought from their parents, who may need a guarantee that participation in the research is without risk for their children. Students should be assured of anonymity and confidentiality throughout the research process, and of their right to withdraw from the research at any stage, should they wish to do so, without any adverse consequences. Other participants, such as colleagues, critical friends and members of your validation group, also need to give consent if they are going to provide feedback during your research and should have the same guarantees of confidentiality, anonymity (if they wish) and right of withdrawal.

If you are undertaking research in your classroom outside of an academic setting, then it is a good idea to examine the *Ethical Guidelines for Educational Research*, published by the British Educational Research Association (BERA, 2018) and follow those guidelines. We advise that readers be aware that ethical expectations may differ in various jurisdictions.

Keeping a record such as that outlined in the Figure 4.1 will help to ensure that you do not overlook any of the permissions or consents required, thus enabling you to engage in good ethical practice. It would also be prudent to include in your ethical considerations, details such as who will have access to your data, where the data will be stored and for how long it will be retained. When you have completed your research, you may wish to share what has been learned with participants and their parents (if appropriate). If you plan to disseminate your research findings more widely, either in oral or written format, it would be a good idea to obtain permission in advance from participants and parents of students. This would help to avoid any ethical dilemmas at a later stage.

	Yes	No	Under way
Permission from college/university	—	—	—
Permission from school authorities or other authorities who need to give permission for you to conduct research	—	—	—
Assent from student participants	—	—	—
If students are minors, permission from their parents	—	—	—
Consent from colleagues/critical friends/validation group	—	—	—
Permission from college/university	—	—	—
Permission from school authorities or other authorities who need to give permission for you to conduct research	—	—	—

Figure 4.1 Checklist of ethical requirements

Attitude towards participants

When the participants in the research are children, they should never be regarded as mere objects of your research. It is important therefore to bear in mind that you are conducting your research *with* your students, not *on* them. This is where your ontological values come to the fore. Framing your research within values such as respect, social justice, equity and inclusion could guide you towards a view that the role of students should be that of co-researchers who can make a valuable contribution to the research in terms of their genuine commitment, enthusiastic participation and honest feedback. Bradbury-Jones and Taylor (2015) suggest that regarding students as co-researchers can have many benefits for the students, for example it has the potential to increase their confidence, enhance their critical thinking skills and promote a sense of empowerment.

Another benefit of a more democratic and life-affirming approach that considers students as co-researchers is the consequent diminution of power in the relationship between you as researcher and your student participants. It is very easy to end up in a situation where you as the researcher possess all the power and retain total control over the research, making all the decisions and using your own ideas and opinions as you formulate your own conclusions. Such a hegemonic approach is disrespectful to the participants, deprives them of a voice in the research process and treats them as objects of the research. You can disrupt this disempowerment of your students by regarding them as co-researchers right from the start of your research. This will ensure that their voices will be heard and that they can experience authentic participation in the research, rather than being mere sources of data.

Making effective use of your data

You should aim to make the most effective use of your data as you engage in your data analysis. It can often be difficult to judge how much data you need to collect. Some researchers err on the side of gathering too little data and then they may discover that they have insufficient data to corroborate their research findings and that, as a result, their research lacks substance. On the other hand, having too much data can leave the researcher feeling overwhelmed and struggling to analyse adequately all the data collected. So how do you avoid these two extremes? A good approach would be to have a specific plan in mind in relation to the purpose of each data collection tool. Then, as you engage in your data collection, ask yourself, "Is this relevant to the aims and purpose of my research? Will this data provide evidence for my research claim?" You will then be able to discern an alignment between the aims of your research and each piece of data that you have gathered. This will lead to a more effective and more efficient approach to data collection, thus avoiding a random or haphazard approach that could cause difficulty at the data analysis stage of your research. Reflection will play a big role here too: it can often happen that, in thinking back over conversations with colleagues, parents or students you will realise that these are vital pieces of data. Figure 4.2 is a checklist to support you in gathering data:

Ongoing Tasks	Yes	No	Under way
Check all necessary ethical permissions are in place	——	——	——
Begin data collection and store carefully	——	——	——
Take note of instances of improved practice and living closely to your values	——	——	——
If data is not indicating improved practice, why is this?	——	——	——
Be aware of any surprising data that might emerge	——	——	——
Organise semi-formal meetings with critical friends and share emergent ideas with them	——	——	——
Complete data collection on time, if possible	——	——	——

Writing Tasks	Yes	No	Under way
Write a paragraph outlining your data collection strategies and why you have chosen them. (As a draft section on methodology for a report)	——	——	——
Write a paragraph beginning with 'I can see that I am enhancing my practice because …'. If this is not the case, write about what you are learning about yourself and your practice in the process. (This may be useful in the findings section of your report)	——	——	——
Write a paragraph beginning with 'I can see that I am enhancing my practice because …'. If this is not the case, write about what you are learning about yourself and your practice in the process. (This may be useful in the findings section of your report)	——	——	——

Figure 4.2 Tasks to assist with data gathering

Section 2: A teacher's experience of collecting data

In this section, we will explore the stories from Aisling, a teacher who shares her experiences of data gathering while doing educational action research in her classroom.

Aisling takes on a challenge that many teacher researchers encounter – finding data in settings where they are working with young or vulnerable participants. The example below is based on Aisling's work as an Early Years primary teacher who investigates how she might adapt her practice in language instruction to align it more with her values. She identified her ontological values as "the importance of life-long and active learning, compassion and understanding," and her epistemological belief "that all learners are knowledge creators" (Connaughton 2021, p. iii). The research took place in an Irish-Language early-immersion setting. She was working in an all-Irish language school and teaching 32 children aged 4–5 years whose first language was English. The data collected shows her account of both her professional and personal learning journeys. She also found data to evaluate the children's understanding of their roles as language learners.

> *Before deciding on an intervention, I gathered data about my current practice from my reflective journal; my pre-existing teaching plans; reflections on whether those plans worked or not, from my students; and from discussions with a learning partner and some others. Critical friends and critical observers in this research were colleagues and other professionals within and outside of my school. All critical friends had experience in education settings, and some had educational research experience. Each of them volunteered to participate with no incentives for participation. A colleague (and learning partner) was invited to observe how I taught language at the outset of the research. As I examined pre-existing teaching plans, I tried to identify areas in which my values of active learning and positioning the learner as a knowledge creator were or were not present. I collected pictures which my children drew of their understanding of their role in language acquisition. I discussed these pictures with critical friends and these discussions were recorded and later transcribed.*

These initial data-gathering approaches incorporated a variety of perspectives and different lenses (Brookfield 2017, p. 7) to show Aisling's practice prior to the research. In summary, she set up a reflective journal to "follow the process of [her] thinking and learning" (Sullivan *et al.* 2016, p. 80). Pre-intervention discussions with critical friends, supervisor and learning partner helped to clarify her planned intervention. A further range of data-collecting methods and the reason for their use are discussed in the final section of this chapter.

The research intervention consisted of three fluid research cycles, each dependent and structured upon the critical reflections of the previous one.

> *In Research Cycle 1, language teaching in the classroom was based on a thematic approach to learning instead of a subject-based approach. Teaching plans were developed to support this, and I critically reflected on the teaching and learning that occurred during this time. Cycle 2 embraced active and experiential language learning in the classroom where I critically reflected on the teaching and learning that occurred and how my values could be seen through my practice. Cycle 3 sought opportunities to learn and use language when engaging with nature and the outdoor environment. I specifically focused on how my teaching was adapted in line with this approach. Critical reflection in this cycle was on the impact of this approach on teaching methodologies and on the children's language acquisition.*

> *Data collected during the cycles included:*
>
> - *My reflective journal*
> - *Reflections on discussions - with critical friends, critical observers and learning partner - added to the validation process*
> - *New teaching plans to incorporate a thematic approach in this early immersion context*
> - *Reflections on feedback from my observations and from critical observers and my learning partner. Throughout this research, I observed the children and, with their collaboration, adapted my plans to support their language learning in a meaningful way.*
> - *Children's new drawings and oral recording of their descriptions. The drawings provided the children's self-report data because "Visualisation can serve as a powerful tool in eliciting subjective experiences and views" (İnözü 2017, p. 2). The recordings, which were transcribed, illuminated the layers of new meanings in their drawings.*

The data collected was qualitative. By engaging with various participants in the research process, their range of lenses (Brookfield 2017, p. 15) added to the validity, reliability and rigour of this research by often challenging taken-for-granted assumptions. Her data collection methods enabled Aisling to claim to have met Winter's (1996) seminal six criteria for rigour in research which are "i) reflexive critique, ii) dialectic critique, iii) collaboration, iv) risking disturbance, v) creating plural structures and vi) theory and practice internalised" (p. 13). This is how these standards of research rigour may be seen in her research:

i   and ii Dialectical and reflexive critique: through exploring her own assumptions and engaging with critical friends, critical observers, a learning partner, reflexive journaling and discussing the research with her validation group

ii   Collaboration by taking everyone's view into consideration and by gathering data from a range of multiple sources.

iii   Risk: by opening the research to the critique of others. She also was open to the risk that her values may not be seen clearly in her practice or that aspects of her research plan may not work.

iv   Plural structure: by gathering data from various participants in the research and by using a cyclical process of action research.

v   Theory/practice transformation: through engaging in multiple developmental cycles, she identified how she could transform her practice. Gradually she showed the theoretically sound foundation of the research as she generated her own living-educational-theory.

Aisling's research was conducted as part of an accredited programme, so the ethical approval occurred in the following ways. Initially she got conditional permission from the

School Head to conduct research into her classroom practice. Following an information letter to the school's Board of Management outlining her research aim, methodology and methods of data collection, she received consent from them also. In the information letter she explicitly discussed that the research was based on her practice and not on the participants themselves. She confirmed to all stakeholders and participants that the identities of the school and the pupils would remain anonymous, and that all data would be collected and stored in accordance with college guidelines and school policies. Next, she submitted the required ethical approval form to the awarding college.

> *Ethical approval was granted for the research, and permission was given by the School Head for me to send information letters to the parents and children to give consent and assent. To aid the children's understanding of the research, I requested that the parents/guardians discussed the research with their children before I asked for their assent in the classroom. Their assent was recorded through putting their fingerprints/identification mark/writing their names on a letter. I organised the secure storage of all data in accordance with the college's requirements. All electronic data was secured using passwords/encryption/access logs and backup, with appropriate firewalls, anti-virus software was in place. All manual data was kept in a locked press. Data was not stored on mobile devices. All participants were made aware of the right to access their personal data and were provided with a copy upon request. The ethical form included that all data would be destroyed appropriately after the storage period. Also, the children would be made aware of the research process and their parents would receive updates on what was happening in the research through an online platform (Seesaw).*

Ethical action research requires more than administrative form filling and storage. Sullivan *et al.* (2016, p. 95) remind us that it consists of "research with people, not on people" so Aisling's methodology adopted an ethical position towards her participants that was based on the values she held.

> *I clarified with all participants what their roles might be. My learning partner colleagues provided me with critical feedback about the approach, their learning and the children's learning. Similarly critical friends and critical observers provided feedback on their learning, their observations and how they perceived the children's learning. These adult participants critically engaged with the research findings and questioned assumptions that may be found. I confirmed that there were no incentives or rewards given for participation. I explained the ethical need to deal with issues of vulnerability, power dynamics, and sensitivity.*

We will consider how and why one might deal with these issues in the final section of this chapter.

In the analysis of data, Aisling employed some quantitative approaches. She developed tables of the frequency of Irish language use in children's depictions of themselves as language learners as she engaged in thematic analysis (Braun and Clarke 2006). In line with her values of active learning and knowledge creation capabilities she analysed the qualitative data collected to identify themes and subthemes that she recognised throughout her research.

Two major themes with sub-themes were identified, all of which were underpinned by my values

1   *Impact of the intervention on learners:*
    - *child participants' perceptions of themselves as language learners*
    - *children's language use*
2   *Impact of the intervention on my self-understanding as a teacher*
    - *realising new values*
    - *challenging assumptions*
    - *living to my values as a language teacher*

Aisling's data collection was designed to suit her specific context and to suit her understanding of what it means to be a teacher in that context. She was creative in finding ways to show what was happening in her practice so that others could understand and critique what she was doing. In the next section we will look at some theories behind why such approaches to data collection are important.

Section 3: A look at why data is collected in these ways

In order to understand why we collect data in ways described so far in this chapter, we can ask why:

- is it important for all researchers to be aware of the ethical issues pertaining to data collection before beginning the research?
- is data collected from the following sources: your own reflective journal and verified conversations with colleagues/parents and participants?
- do student teachers collect data during their practicum?
- does each data collection tool have a specific purpose?
- do we mine data?

In this section of the chapter, we will address these questions.

Ethical issues in data collection

We begin by considering why it is important for all researchers to be aware of the ethical issues pertaining to data collection before beginning the research. Research ethics provide guidelines that support researchers in conducting research so that it is done justly, and without harming anyone in the process (Hickey 2018, np). Therefore, it is important for all researchers to be aware of the ethical issues around data collection before beginning the research. Before you collect data, you must establish and plan how you will follow the ethical guidelines. This will form part of your research report. In the case of accredited research, all the ethical guidelines of the institution must be adhered to.

It may be helpful to think about what we mean by ethics. Yoak and Brydon-Miller (2014, p. 306) say that ethics are about what we value in our relationships with others and with the physical world and "how we put values into action" in the decisions we make. Hilsen (2006, p. 27) explains what such definitions may mean for researchers as "the unconditional responsibility and the ethical demand to act in the best interests of our fellow human beings." Our fellow human beings include participants, observers, critical friends and others involved in the research. The idea of acting in their best interest encompasses both enhancing our practice and showing the impact of our research on participants and settings. Impact is not necessarily a quantitative measure but as McNiff *et al.* (2018, p. 803) argue, in ethical action research, impact means "that we have had an educative influence and the practice of shared expertise in our research." We will explain the idea of educational influence further in Chapter 6.

University and department ethical committees set ethical requirements for the research they accredit, but regardless of whether your research is accredited or not, ethics in action research is broader than getting informed consent from all gatekeepers and participants to collect data and store it. When writing about research ethics, you may state how your values influence your ethical responsibilities towards participants. This will include actions such as debriefing them when the research is completed and having their permission to make public their contributions to your research. As we have said earlier, making your research public and understandable by others is a key feature of demonstrating the educational influence of your research. Permission for this can be obtained before the research begins such as when "parents were asked to agree that their child's work could be used as part of the research and were invited to view any data that C [the researcher] planned to make public" (McDonagh *et al.* 2020, p. 109).

The idea of gathering data *with* participants rather than *from* participants demonstrates values of "respect for people and for the knowledge and experience they bring to the research process" (Brydon-Miller *et al.* 2003, p. 15). In the research example in Section 2, Aisling acknowledged this, yet she identified issues of power dynamics, sensitivity and vulnerability when dealing with young pupils in classroom research. We will now consider these issues.

The imbalance of power between teacher and student should not be ignored. You might involve a range of people (special needs assistants, classroom assistants, other teachers, involved professionals and therapists, principal, parents, etc.), as well as your students, to validate that your findings are fair and balanced. Likewise, to avoid a possible power imbalance when dealing with critical feedback from all adult participants, you might consider anonymised responses and feedback so that it could be given honestly. You should also make sure that all participants are aware that they can opt out of the research at any point and make it clear that there are no consequences for their participation or non-participation in the research.

Sensitivity may be shown in your classroom research by considering the possibility that occasionally participants may make a disclosure of a child protection issue. If a child protection issue arises, then the proper steps must be taken, and appropriate authorities informed immediately. Another sensitive aspect might be that the school context or the research project itself might be stressful for the students. This was identified in Section 2 when Aisling collected data sensitively from her pupils by using visual and oral methods which mitigated against any stress they may feel in their early language immersion context.

Young children in classroom research are considered to be a vulnerable group. In Ireland, for example, the Department of Children and Youth Affairs (2017, p. 31) states that those conducting research activities with children have statutory responsibilities to children and young people with regard to education and research. Researchers who are researching their own practice may also be vulnerable to personal and professional risks involved in reflecting critically (Brookfield 2017). Dialogue and peer support groups may help you to navigate such difficulties.

Dialogue and conversations as a data collection tool

We will now consider why data is collected from the following sources: your own reflective journal and verified conversations with colleagues, parents and participants. Your journal is a dialogue or conversation with yourself. When you make a record of a conversation during your research and ask those participating to verify if your record is accurate, you now have data in the form of a verified conversation. Bear in mind that your journal will form part of your data archive which may be examined, if doing formal research. Student teachers might be obliged to keep their reflective journals in an e-portfolio which is open to viewing by module or course leaders, tutors, supervisors and external examiners.

Reflective journals and transcripts from conversations with others form part of critical reflection practices. As we explained in Chapter 2, reflecting on one's educational practice has become an integral part of teachers' professional development in recent times, particularly since Schön produced his seminal work on this topic, which was followed up by further explication of his ideas in 1995. In developing his theories around reflection, Schön claims to have been influenced by the tradition of reform initiated by Rousseau, Dewey, Vygotsky, Lewin and Piaget, among others. His ideas centred around the dual phenomenon of reflection-in-action and reflection-on-action, both of which will be evident in your reflective journaling.

According to Schön, reflection-in-action occurs when professional practitioners think about what they are doing, while they are doing it. Their reflections create new understandings of their actions leading to new knowledge of their practice. They are in essence conducting research in their practice context. Schön suggests that reflection-in-action can influence the outcome of the action, when he states: "The actor reflects 'in action' in the sense that his thinking occurs in an action-present—a stretch of time within which it is still possible to make a difference to the outcomes of the action" (1995, p. 30). Practitioners reflect on their actions while engaging in the actions and can alter the actions as a result of their reflections, thus producing different outcomes to what may have been intended initially. This would be a useful strategy for you as you carry out your research. It is not something that comes naturally to everyone, but with practice you will find that thinking within the action is a good skill to cultivate.

Reflection-on-action is done retrospectively, after the action has occurred. The time constraint that could possibly be a limiting factor for the practice of reflection-in-action is not an issue here. There is, therefore, greater opportunity for deeper reflection *on* one's actions. Critical reflection will enable the practitioner to identify aspects that may not have gone according to plan, or that have not had the desired effect. The practitioner can then establish why the plan did not work; learn from the process; restructure the plan; and put the revised plan into operation in their practice. In effect, the practitioner is engaging with the main stages of an action research cycle: plan, act, observe and reflect, which is long established, for example, in Carr and Kemmis (1986) and Cohen *et al.* (2018). The process of constant reflection and changing of plans will lead to improvement in your practice, greater understanding of your practice, and more enhanced learning about yourself and your practice.

We authors now consider the renaming of these concepts as reflection-in-practice and reflection-on-practice because we feel that they might more accurately represent the kind of reflection we do in educational action research. By engaging in these two kinds of reflections you can gather valuable data for the purpose of your research (Sullivan *et al.* 2016). We have discussed previously the importance of keeping a research journal in which to record and dialogue with your actions and your reflections on your actions. Details of your reflections on your practice should be included in your journal. You could then, at a later stage, reflect on your initial reflections, in a process of meta-reflection, which will allow for deeper introspection into your thoughts and actions. Your reflections and meta-reflections will be rich sources of data for you when you need to provide evidence of your research findings as you analyse your data. In Glenn *et al.* (2017, p. 13), we write how, as we became involved in a professional conversation group, we saw "knowledge emerge in the conversations we had with colleagues; in our attempts to express our ideas and in our listening to others. We found our learning to be socially constructed." Glenn recalls in her reflective journal that "our learning is stimulated as we speak and listen, where communication and dialogue is the scaffolding of our learning" (Shulman 1999, cited in Glenn *et al.* 2017 p. 13).

We will now examine links between critically reflective practice and data collection. Reflection, whether *in* or *on* practice, needs to have a critical element to it in order to be truly effective. It is not a matter of taking a quick look at what you have been doing and then moving on quickly to the next action. It involves taking a step back and asking probing questions. It means interrogating your own interpretations and assumptions in relation to your actions. Brookfield (2017) suggests that practitioners can critically reflect on their practice by examining their assumptions through four complementary lenses: their own views, the opinions of their students, the perceptions of their colleagues and the theories in the research literature. Using all four lenses will help to alert you to any aspects of your research that may need further investigation. As well as your own interpretation of your practice, you will have an external perspective from the other lenses which will provide you with a more accurate understanding of your research. The critical insights gained from using the various lenses, and written up in your journal will become valuable data that will assist you in adding rigour, validity and authenticity to your research data.

Data collection and student teachers

Do student teachers collect data during their practicum? This depends on the structure of their teacher education programme. In Ireland, all student teachers are required to con-duct independent research as part of their teacher-education programme (Brennan 2019). This means that they must "engage in data gathering and critically analyse and evaluate relevant knowledge and research" (Teaching Council 2017, p.27). Furthermore, all Initial Teacher Education (ITE) programmes in Ireland include "teacher as researcher" as a core element that should underpin all aspects of programmes of ITE (Teaching Council 2017, p.14). During a practicum or placement in schools in most teacher education courses, students reflect on and record aspects of their practice. Other courses require various research elements, for example, in the *Student Teacher Educational Research (STER) Report,* Brennan (2019) tells how students, who shared their research in a student-led peer learning community, gained "a greater appreciation for the potential of educational re-search to influence practice" (p. 44). Classroom-based research projects are part of initial teacher education in many countries including India, Canada and Europe (Agud and Ion 2019; Chiennat 2015).

As we said earlier, teaching offers a broad range of data-gathering possibilities. As a student teacher your data sources are plentiful, although they may be more limited by time constraints than other educators. For this reason, it is worth repeating that it is imperative that you design a manageable research plan. Student teachers will have access to their own teaching notes; observations; reflections on lessons; comments from the classroom teacher and examiners; pupils' reactions and comments and so on.

Data gathered through dialogue and collaborative conversations has significance for student teachers as well as for teachers throughout their careers (see Glenn *et al.* 2017). Gathering data from dialogue can enhance the rigour and authenticity of the research. In addition, collaborative conversations have a key function in lifelong professional devel-opment and also have implications for time-constrained research and for student-teacher research.

When teachers' research is not conducted for accreditation or for school or systemic evaluation, the importance of gathering information from dialogue and collaborative dis-cussion is self-evident. In time-constrained research, such as that often conducted by stu-dent teachers, this aspect is currently often limited, or omitted, to the detriment of the research. In discussions and dialogues, new meanings are created between the participants. This data does not exist independently of the discussions but is created as the parties try to clarify and make meaning from what they individually bring to the discussion. Audio recording, video recording and transcribing (with appropriate permissions in place) of such collaborative discussions can add to the validation of research claims and findings. Validation will be explained further in the next chapter.

Identifying the specific purpose for each data collection tool

Your research setting and its ethos will help you address the question, "does each data collection tool have a specific purpose?" Knowing your own context and its culture will make it easy to justify why you have chosen particular data collection tools. Clarity around the purpose of each data collection tool is important. This means that you must check regularly that the data you are collecting is relevant to your research question as well as to the values you hold. It should tell you about your work in your area of interest or concern and consequently, that of your values.

We will take some time now to explore how you might explain the specific purpose of dialogue as a research tool. Traditionally not recognised as a research tool, dialogue has now become a widely used tool in the field of educational action research. Delong (2020) argues that dialogue as a research tool has evolved to the point that it is now the significant means "by which I describe and explain the nature of my educational influence in my own learning, in the learning of others and in the learning of social formations and create accounts of my own living-educational-theories" (p. 71). Many other educational and social researchers have likewise attested to the vital role that dialogue and professional conversations play in improving professional practice, professional relationships and even teacher well-being (Burbules 2000; Clark 2001; Glenn *et al.* 2017; Irvine and Price 2014; Lummis *et al.* 2022 among many others).

To explain why researchers put time into analysing conversations that take place during their research, we look again to the epistemological and ontological values of researchers. Massó-Guijarro (2021) examined the potential of dialogue for education, learning and social transformation. He concluded that "dialogical education allows the development of innovative communicative strategies that promote intersubjective teaching-learning, the encounter with the other, the appreciation of difference" (Massó-Guijarro 2021, p. 85). By including data from dialogues, researchers are conducting research in an educational way that demonstrates how knowledge is generated and transferred. It also shows that we value the professional knowledge of colleagues and the personal and experiential knowledge of all participants. This is an inclusive form of data gathering which enables researchers to demonstrate values of integrity, honesty and reliability.

Figure 4.3 summarises the purposes of data collection and shows them as a developmental, incremental process. It shows the progression from checking what sources of data are available to you to how your data can provide evidence to validate the claim you make for your research. As part of this process you demonstrate that your data will help you to address your research question. A key element in educational action research is to check that data offers both you, the teacher researcher and your participants possibilities for having your voices heard which is. Your research methods will describe and explain how each of your activities and reflections influence the next step and also how they influence your learning and the learning of others.

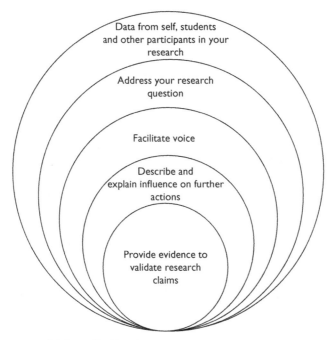

Figure 4.3 Purposes of data collection here

Many who research their practice, begin to analyse what has been learned when they develop a framework into which items of data can be placed. We would like to introduce this framework (Figure 4.4) to help you analyse your data. They are examples of enhanced practice, new insights into practice and links between your values and your practice. Mining your data means digging deeply into it to unearth and expose examples of enhanced practice, new insights into practice and links between your values and your practice (Figure 4.4). (We will

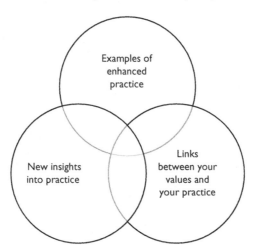

Figure 4.4 Framework for data analysis

discuss this in further detail as we examine how we extrapolate evidence from the data in Chapter 5.) Very often these three areas are interlinked and provide us with the new learning that emerges in the research process.

It also means developing explanations from the array of data you have collected. Your data gathering was part of a living process. This fluidity has provided you with descriptions of what happened during the research. You may now begin to generate theory from your practice as you begin to outline the story of your learning from the research process, in terms of descriptions and explanations (Whitehead and McNiff 2006). As you begin to explain to yourself and others, what was learned in the research, decide on a date to cease data collection.

Conclusion

To summarise, your initial data collection can provide a clear and brief picture of your work so that others can understand your research setting and the research question you have formulated. Your data will show that it is an honest account of your situation. As your research progresses you will find ways of demonstrating change in your thinking and improvement in your practice. The importance of collecting data ethically was explained in Sections 1 and 3. This enables you to show that you have conducted your research rigorously and honestly alongside your co-researchers/participants. In this chapter we showed how you might begin to collect data and we explained the importance of honest, ethical and trustworthy data-collection tools.

In the next chapter, we look at how you can move from a collection of data to making a claim that you have learned something new from your research and have generated your personal living theory of practice.

Additional reading suggestions

Clark, C. (2001) (ed) *Talking Shop: Authentic Conversation and Teacher Learning.* New York: Teachers College Press.

Glenn, M., Roche, M., McDonagh, C. and Sullivan, B. (2017) *Learning Communities in Educational Partnerships*, London and New York: Bloomsbury. Chapter 2

Sullivan, B., Glenn, M., Roche, M., McDonagh, C. (2016) *Introduction to Critical Reflection and Action for Teacher Researchers.* Abingdon: Routledge.

Suggested resources

Rose, N. (2015) 'Ethical issues in teacher-led research', *Evidence into Practice: a blog about evidence-informed teaching*, available: https://evidenceintopractice.wordpress.com/2015/04/05/ethical-issues-in-teacher-led-research/ [accessed 1 May 2022].

Delong, J. (2022) 'Dialogue as a research method', *Jackie Delong in Conversation*, [video], available: https://youtu.be/HUKJsYbYGtU, [accessed 28 January 2023].

5 Presenting evidence: Values as research standards

This chapter is about evidence. Evidence means presenting your data in ways to show that what you have learned during your research is valid. This is done in order to provide an honest, fair and ethical account of the research that can be substantiated. We will show how you can strengthen your research by establishing your own standards of judgement and evaluating if you have, in fact, met these standards or not.

Throughout this book you are working towards giving an account of your research into your practice that is based on the values that you hold. The standards of judgement for your research will be drawn from these values (Whitehead and McNiff 2006) and will help you to evaluate the quality and integrity of your claim to knowledge. The sections in this chapter will show how to present evidence, how a teacher researcher provided evidence of a claim to new knowledge and the importance of validating your research claim and generating a living theory.

The chapter shows how you might present evidence to support your new learning in the following ways:

- by establishing standards that are drawn from your values
- by assessing whether you are meeting the standards that you have established
- by presenting your new learning to a validation group to establish if your claim is honest and valid
- by showing how knowledge creation can be a value and a source of validation as you develop your living-educational-theory from researching your practice

Section 1: Presenting evidence and showing your values as research standards

To explain the process simply, you can begin by revisiting the data that you have collected (see Chapter 4) and asking yourself if it shows your values in action, and if you can demonstrate that you have created new knowledge from undertaking your research. You can then present your new learning claims to others, for example your validation group, who can validate your claims if you can demonstrate that they are rigorous. Continue the ongoing tasks of journaling, reflecting and reading that you have established in earlier chapters. In this chapter, we now add dialogue as an ongoing feature of your research process.

DOI: 10.4324/9781003288183-6

In the previous chapter, we discussed a variety of forms of data collection, which you could then use to provide evidence of your new learning from conducting your research. This new learning can constitute your research claim. When we talk about new learning, we are using this term in the broadest sense. It could be new learning about your professional practice as an educator, or it could be about your efforts to live to your educational values. Your new learning could be related to your students and how they negotiate the pedagogical relationships in your classroom. It might also be around the fact that you now have a greater understanding of your practice – or it might be something you have not anticipated at all. Begin by examining your journal and your reflections on your practice for the specific purpose of unearthing anything that constitutes new learning for you in the course of carrying out your research. It is worth initially writing these claims, so that you can reword and refine them as you work through the process of presenting evidence.

At this stage of your research, you need to revisit your data so that you can scrutinise it and evaluate it in terms of how it relates to your research standards. An effective and rigorous method of doing so may be to take Brookfield's (2017) four lenses for critical reflection, as discussed in Chapters 2 and 4, and adapt them for the purpose of examining your data. These lenses are your own perspective, your students' views, feedback from colleagues and theories in the literature. Your own views can be gleaned from scrutinising your reflective journal, in which you will have recorded the story of your learning through your reflections on your actions and thoughts throughout the research process. The views of your students, which you may have gathered through discussions with them, questionnaires or focus groups, should provide you with evidence of new learning. Colleagues and critical friends may corroborate, or challenge, your own interpretations of your data. Looking at the theories in the literature can provide evidence that supports, or contradicts, your findings from your research.

Standards of judgement drawn from your values

In an academic setting, the account of your research needs to meet certain standards in order to be considered good quality research. If you are undertaking your research as part of an accredited course, your institution will have standards that your research report has to achieve. In an educational action research project, in addition to the standards established by your institution, you can also use standards of judgement based on your values to evaluate your research. If you are conducting your research outside of an academic course, you might likewise want to show that your research is authentic, rigorous and valid, so you can use standards of judgement based on your values to evaluate your research. Whitehead and McNiff (2006) differentiate between criteria, which they describe as markers of performance, and standards of judgement, which relate to the quality of the research. The standards of judgement can be based on your ontological and epistemological values.

You can establish these standards at the beginning of your research, when you begin to state your values. You will then be able to ascertain, during the course of your research, whether or not you appear to be achieving these standards. If you inform other participants in your research of your standards at the outset, they will be able to monitor your values-based standards of judgement throughout the research process. An example of establishing a standard of judgement might be:

Amy is a teacher of six-year-olds. She is concerned because many of the pupils seem disinterested and are weak at reading. She values lifelong learning and feels reading is an important part of that process. Her research question is "How might I improve my teaching of reading so that my pupils can become active agents in the course of their own learning?" She establishes two standards of judgement for her research which are linked with her values. These are: (1) Can I identify occasions when children are enjoying reading? and (2) Are there occasions when the children use books to enhance their learning process? She will use these standards as indicators that she is living more closely to her values and enhancing her practice in the teaching of reading.

Meeting research standards of judgement

Having other people to corroborate your claim that you have met your research standards adds rigour and validity to your research findings. Let's look at how this might work in practice. Suppose, for example, that one of your educational values is inclusion. Your standards based on this value might be "Have I demonstrated inclusion in my classroom practice?" You could then monitor your practice to see if there are instances where all students have been included in a meaningful way in classroom activities. Such incidents could be recorded in your reflective journal and form part of your data collection. Your students may be able to cite instances where they experienced inclusion in the classroom. Colleagues and critical friends could also check for occasions where they have noticed the practice of inclusionary measures in your classroom. They would then have evidence to state that you have met the standard of inclusion in your research. You could apply a similar process to other standards drawn from your values that you wish to be used in assessing your research, thus ensuring stringency and rigour in articulating your findings.

Sometimes, teacher researchers find that they do not meet their established standards and they feel disheartened. As they explore why this might have happened, they will gain new insight into their practice and establish new learning. This might even form an important new cycle in the research process.

Establishing a validation group

Your research findings can be strengthened further by establishing a validation group. You can set up a validation group specifically for the purpose of providing rigour and authenticity for your research. The validation group can consist of pre-existing critical friends, colleagues, fellow researchers and people who would be familiar with the research methodology and with your area of enquiry. The purpose of setting up this group is so that you can present an account of your research to them. They will then assess your research in terms of whether your data supports your claim to have developed new learning about your practice. The validation group will adopt a critical approach in evaluating your research and may challenge your interpretation of events. They will also be able to judge whether you have presented sufficient evidence to show that your practice has been enhanced and that you have lived to your values in the course of your research. In Section 2, you will see how a teacher researcher set up and managed a validation group.

Knowledge creation and your living educational theory

The new knowledge that you have created from your research can be expressed as a theory of your educational practice. You will have encountered several theories in the literature that you have accessed during the course of your research and that have influenced both your thinking and your approach to carrying out your research. The theory that evolves from the process of doing your research is a practical theory, emanating from your educational practice. It is a living theory, arising out of the lived reality of your experience of living to your values. Because of your commitment to enact your values in your practice, the theory that you develop from your actions can be considered your living theory. We draw on the work of Whitehead (2018) here. The descriptions and explanations that you have provided for your research will contribute to the formation of your living educational theory. If you can demonstrate that your research has had a positive impact in your learning, and in the learning of others, you can claim to have met the requirements for a living theory, which Whitehead (2018, p. 70) describes as "an explanation produced by an individual for their educational influence in their own learning, in the learning of others, and in the learning of the social formation in which they live and work."

Here we summarise some tasks (Figure 5.1) you can undertake to help you generate evidence:

Ongoing Tasks	Yes	No	Under Way
Continue journaling and examine your journal for instances of anything that constitutes new learning	—	—	—
Reflect on your data sources and how they relate to your values	—	—	—
Read theories in the literature and consider their relevance to your research	—	—	—
Continue to talk to critical friends	—	—	—
Presenting evidence tasks			
Name some validation criteria /standards of judgement drawn from your values	—	—	—
Comb through the data for incidents where you are meeting your criteria/standards of judgement where you can see how you are living to your values and how you are enhancing your practice – or not.	—	—	—
Take note of any other incidents of interest. Name your claims to new learning for yourself, participants and others.t	—	—	—
Set up a validation group and schedule meetings with them and critical friends	—	—	—
Writing tasks			
Plan questions for critical friend(s) and validation group meetings.	—	—	—
Make agreed notes from all validation meetings	—	—	—

Figure 5.1 Validation tasks

Section 2: An example of how one teacher generated theory in an educational action research project

Here is Greg's story as he researched "How do I Nurture Compassion in my Classroom?" (Joynt 2019). His values which he used as standards for judging his research were respect, inclusivity, compassion and social justice. The research took place in a primary, co-educational, urban school with a prosperous socio-economic background, where academic achievement was highly valued and prioritised. He realised that his role needed to go beyond academic instruction by also actively nurturing caring and compassionate relationships in the classroom, in line with his values. The descriptions of his validation process show how he monitored his practice to see if there were instances where his values were demonstrated in a meaningful way. The story begins with the setting up of a validation group:

Starting a validation group

My validation group consisted of a member of the school Special Education Team of teachers who regularly did in-class support with my class, two colleagues who had my class previously and a teacher in another school. My supervisor also provided validation for my data, findings and claims.

Four weeks into my research the group had our first meeting. We discussed two questions about the data I had collected. First, did I have enough data, which we called data saturation? The second question related to the validity of my research with young children: did they really learn from taking part in my investigation of how I taught, or were they merely going along with what they thought that I wanted them to say? The latter is called acquiescence. During our discussions, the validation group helped me to identify any gaps in the research. I recorded their feedback in my journal as follows:

1   The validation group agreed that data had reached saturation and that the children appeared to have a good understanding of compassion based on their journal entries, on the group's observations in my class and on my journal.
2   Had acquiescence been obvious to the validation group, it would have shown a power dimension where pupils possibly felt they were being researched by me, as a teacher researcher, rather than participating in my research as co-researchers. In relation to acquiescence, the group commented on the level of honesty in the children's written accounts, the richness of the data and how self-aware the children were in their answers.
3   My validation group provided me with clarity to recognise power dynamics at play between children themselves and teacher/child dynamics through observations of my work.
4   I constantly adjusted my actions and reflections based on the actions of the pupils, and the views of their parents, as well as the perspectives of my colleagues, so that I could get a better understanding of any power dynamics at play.

The first meeting provided evidence of the rigour of Greg's research methodology. He had shown that there was adequate data collection, a developmental cyclical educational action research process, adjustments for the ethical issues of power dynamics that arose, and he developed clarity about his research through engaging in meaningful conversations with the validation group. His standards of judgement of respect, inclusivity and social justice were explicit and alive in this validation process.

Developing valid claims to new knowledge

> During my second research cycle, I met with my validation group again, to show my findings based on my data and to provide an opportunity for them to critique my claims.
>
> The group noted that the data provided evidence that the children had developed a deeper understanding of compassion.
>
> They identified how I increasingly used the perspectives of the children and of others before taking further research actions.
>
> My validation group discussed possible claims to knowledge that I could make based on my research. We discussed generalising my intervention in other classes and they noted that the successful enactment of the intervention hinged on the teacher's own levels of compassion and that was what made it an authentic experience for the class.

The second group meeting examines the validity of Greg's methodological approach and his claims. In this final piece from his research, Greg explains how his research had had an influence in his own learning, in the learning of others and in the learning of social formations. This influence is a key requirement of generating a living educational theory of your practice, as we will explain in the final section of this chapter.

What Greg learned from his research

> I have been inspired to compose my own definition of compassion having lived the experience of nurturing compassion in my classroom.
>
> Compassion is using and acknowledging perspectives, recognising our shared human connection and acting in ways to resolve the suffering of others and oneself. Compassion requires imagination, practice and courage.
>
> During my research I learned that compassion proved to be something that can be learnable and nurtured implicitly and explicitly in the classroom. Self-compassion proved to have an important role, not only in the well-being of the child, but also in my well-being as a teacher researcher.
>
> **Influencing the learning of others and social formations in the school**
>
> My influence in the learning of the pupils in my classroom and its validation against the values I held was easily documented in the analysis of the findings of my research.

The reflections written by my validation group (two of which are shared below) provide evidence of my influence in pupils' learning, in colleagues' learning and in the learning of the wider school community.

- A participating pupil's parent wrote "As a parent I would have to say that my daughter showed her learning on compassion through conversations we had. She was most engaged on topics discussed in class and really enjoyed the variety of modes used to learn about compassion. She spoke of the drama games such as forum theatre, conscience alley, cross the line, novel reading, letter writing, walking debates and that is just to mention a few. I know this work will always be of benefit to her."
- A senior colleague who had observed my research actions in my classroom was impressed and wanted others on the staff to learn about it. He particularly wanted new staff members who were Newly Qualified Teachers (NQTs) to experience what was happening and wrote as follows, "I asked the Droichead* coordinator in our school to approach Greg and enquire if our Newly Qualified Teachers (NQTs) could observe his lessons on compassion. Greg readily agreed to this. Our three NQTs reported that they learned so much that afternoon."

---

*Droichead is an integrated professional induction framework for newly qualified teachers (Teaching Council Ireland 2016b).

Greg has taken us through his process of checking his data gathering with others to ensure that his research approach is rigorous. This is important because his data-gathering approaches were creative and diverse. In bringing his data and claims to his validation group, he was utilising a significant feature of educational action research. In his research, there may have been a huge list of findings which included evaluating actions, ideas, thinking, and the learning of all involved in the research. However, these findings were not just written up and discussed in a report. Greg examined his findings for data to show evidence of his claims.

By presenting his standards of judgement and these claims to his validation group, their collaborative expertise, during their recorded discussions, enabled them to assess whether his research was credible, reliable and methodologically rigorous. We will discuss these terms in the final section of the chapter. For now, we can see that Greg's data was tested to see if he had valid claims to new learning which showed his standards of judgement - meaning could his values be seen in action in these claims. His claims, supported by data, were discussed by his validation group and this led to the validation of his research claims.

The group confirmed that the research had an educational effect in that it had an influence in the learning of others. These others were not only the participants in the research but also colleagues in the wider school community. The group acknowledged the authenticity of Greg's research when they recognised that he was living as fully as possible to his values. Whitehead (2021, p. 1) suggests such responses from a validation group demonstrate the validity of living theory action research.

In the final section of this chapter, we discuss why this process is important in educational action research.

Section 3: The importance of validating your research claim and generating a living theory

Often when we are teaching, we have a sense that a class went particularly well or was a flop. We "just know." Previous experiences, and professional skills we have developed, might account for this feeling. But in fact, it is a deeper form of knowing, which is called personal knowledge or tacit knowledge. Though we may have written down some of these successes and failures in a research journal, it is difficult to explain to others how this "gut instinct" is valid evidence of new learning. This is a cause of concern for some researchers, while others also worry that so much of their data comes from their journals and question how it can be seen as valid research.

In this section, we suggest some explanations to show why the findings can result in valid new learning. We discuss generating evidence from the research to create personal knowledge and new learning. We do so by explaining:

- how to establish a robust validation process of your personal and professional new learning
- guidance on validity and ways to show you have met the standards you have established
- why the generation of theory from research in practice is important

Establishing a robust validation process

In the first part of this chapter, we described how one might present evidence in support of your new learning, as in Greg's story above. Now we will explain how to establish a robust validation process.

Your research claim is about what you now know that you didn't know before undertaking your research. Focusing on your own learning is important. You learn by reflecting on your actions and your actions personify your learning. So, when you write a report on your research or make it public in any other way, you must include not only the research processes and actions you took, but also what you learned. If you neglect to report your learning, it "can weaken the authenticity of the research" (McNiff 2010, p. 11).

An explanation of the validation of personal learning and personal knowledge

Gut instinct, personal learning and personal knowledge do not generally feature in traditional research. Yet gut instinct and personal ways of knowing can be kernel in educational action research (McDonagh and Sullivan 2017). Michael Polanyi's work (1958, 1966 and 1969 in particular) suggests a theoretical base that could explain how to value the knowledge created by practitioner researchers' professional and personal gut feelings that seemed so difficult to put into a traditional research framework.

Polanyi's theories on personal knowing, tacit knowing, and knowing and being (Polanyi 1958, 1966 and 1969) provide an understanding of what forms of knowledge are valued as well as how new knowledge is created during our research. Polanyi's ideas of personal or tacit knowledge relate to the forms of knowledge which are not learned facts or skills but are intuitive. Sen (2009, p. xi) in the Foreword to Polanyi's *The Tacit Dimension* (2009) says that when we value tacit and personal knowledge "as part of knowledge in general then we can know 1) what we want to look for, and 2) what else we may want to know." These two ideas support an important feature of educational action research. They allow for the development of a research process, such as we have described in this book, that provides an explanation for educational action research as a research approach – one that does not start from a thesis to be proved but stems from a developmental approach to finding new personal understanding about one's practice.

If we pause for a moment and think about the following ideas in Greg's research report above, we can see another example of Polanyi's ideas in practice. The sentence to focus on is "*They noted that 'the successful enactment of the intervention hinged on the teacher's own levels of compassion and that was what made it an authentic experience for the class.*" The validation group were voicing the importance of Greg's personal and tacit knowledge even though they may never have heard of Polanyi's theories.

As we conduct real-life research on our practice, an awareness of our epistemological value around our personal way of knowing is helpful. Polanyi's theory of knowledge explains the validation of our personal knowledge and we can use it as a theoretical explanation of personal learning from our research.

Now that we have examined the ideas of Polanyi we have an understanding of the value of knowledge and why as educators this is important in educational classroom research. We can use Polanyi's theories to explain and justify why we use evidence of personal knowledge and learning in the validation of our research claims.

Why validity is important

In this section we consider validity and ways to show we have met the standards of judgement drawn from our values. Being rigorous is especially important when researching our practice. Because we are sharing our personal knowledge drawn from critical reflection and from the investigation of our practice, the validation process must be stringent and rigorous (McDonagh 2017). We address this by building in extra validation processes. If we are conducting our research for accreditation, we also abide by academic guidelines. Having explained the importance of tacit and personal knowledge in our real-life research process, we now want to bring this internal and implicit knowledge to the fore, and make it public, so that it can be validated by others.

We authors often cite the work of the philosopher Jurgen Habermas to explain how valid meanings can be arrived at through communicating with others. His *Theory of Communicative Action* (Habermas 1976) shows how we start to make sense of our own personal learning from our research by engaging with others. He proposes that, as humans talking to each other, we are naturally able to agree on decisions. Building on this argument, he suggests, we can transform this ability into well-defined new knowledge.

Habermas says that there are certain conditions or principles necessary to validly ensure new understandings through dialogue. They are that, as a researcher, one must speak comprehensibly, truthfully, authentically and appropriately. Being aware of these standards enables us to present a theoretical base for evidence we produce to show that others have validated our learning from our research.

Here is what Habermas's principles might mean to us as teacher researchers. When we explain our research claim in ways that others can understand we are speaking (or writing) comprehensibly. We speak truthfully when we provide adequate data to enable others to recognise our claims. Letting others understand the life worlds that we are researching demonstrates authenticity and we can help others experience this by giving direct expression to all participants' voices, including our own. The idea of appropriate communication means using appropriate language (McDonagh *et al.* 2020).

We can show that we have met those standards when we discuss our research with others and invite them to critique it. In this way we can claim to have social validity according to Habermas' Theory of Communicative Action (1976). Whitehead and McNiff (2006) state that the social validity of Habermas is clear when the research has "standards to show that my research is credible, truthful, sincere and appropriate" (2006, pp. 141-144). While Habermas published his theory over 40 years ago, it retains its relevance in research validation today, locally and internationally, as in the following recent examples:

Habermas' (1976) theory has been used by Canadian researchers Griffin and Delong (2021, p. 36) to strengthen the personal and social validity of their living educational theories. Griffin, a school principal, and Delong, a retired superintendent of education and international mentor, collaborate to share how Living Educational Theory helped them to improve their practice and transform their lives. They use visual data and dialogue including YouTube clips and transcripts as research methods. They emphasise the relatability of their research study and they want readers to relate what they read and see to the reader's own practice – opening up new dialogues. They cite comprehensibility, truthfulness, rightness and authenticity as their standards in developing their theories through these various forms of dialogue.

Rahman *et al.* (2021) strengthened their research by making their context and educational values clear. When they researched their community of practice in Bangladesh, they developed a transformative, cooperative living educational theory with children and youth. They explained their process of developing authenticity in line with Habermas (1976) and presented the story of their research in a way that is comprehensible and truthful. They say that they "show why we do what we do, critically judge our practice, and provide evidence for our claims to knowledge by making the voices of the people in this research heard" (Rahman *et al.* 2021, p. 33).

Both Greg Joynt's (2019) questions for his validation group in Section 2 above and Whitehead's "Research Planner" (Whitehead n.d.) with its suggested questions for a validation group may give the impression that the validation process is a case of answering defined questions. Validation in educational action research is not a tick-the-box-and-the-job-is-done exercise. It is about clarifying your personal or tacit understandings (see Polanyi 1966) and convincing others (see Habermas 1976). It involves learning together through dialogue. Dialogue with others begins when you first engage with your critical friend(s). You prepare your ideas in your head prior to opening them up to others. Similar to when you tried to articulate and name your values in earlier chapters, your thinking about what you are learning during your research is clarified as you try to explain it to others. As you dialogue with your critical friend(s) you engage in what Glenn *et al.* (2017, p. 16) calls dialogue for clarification. This can further develop into a "dialogue for personal learning" (Glenn *et al.* 2017, p. 17) as you discuss your research approach, data and claims with your validation group and critical friend(s). When you speak with them, together you are wrestling with the meaning (or sometimes the misunderstandings) of what is happening in your research. Just as Habermas's (1976) theory suggests, when you and your validation group, or critical friend(s), try to fully understand what is happening in your research, you are each making new meanings together. You are each learning. You are each engaged in a "dialogue for personal learning" (Glenn *et al.* 2017, p. 17). Every aspect of the process of educational action research is about learning. Therefore, it is an appropriate approach for teachers conducting research in their classrooms.

Generating living theory from your research

We have discussed how we can use theories to explain the validation of the new knowledge you created through your research. It is important that teacher researchers not only absorb and learn from the theory in the literature but that they also learn to generate their own living theories from their classroom practice for a number of reasons. Our practice is often guided and organised according to policy, government requirements and curricula makers. These agencies are often guided by theories from big data research, which while generalisable may not be specific enough for pupils in our classrooms. In the case of the inclusion of pupils with learning difficulties, for example, the advice on best practice may often come from theories based in non-educational disciplines such as medicine, psychology and speech and language therapy. There is a strong need for educational theories by teachers for teachers. We will explain in detail how this can be done in the next chapter.

Throughout this book we have spoken of improving one's practice. Some researchers, however, may fail to identify an improvement in their practice. For example, Carozzi (2019) explains how she developed her journey towards generating her educational theory of her self-enquiry, even though she did not claim a change or improvement in her practice. She did, nonetheless, claim a new understanding of herself and her practice. In analysing her data, which included extracts from her own diaries, private correspondence and written assignments, she told of her struggles to define her practice. It became "an account of an evolving and emerging awareness of my own self, embodied in my own educational development" (Carozzi 2019, p. 39).

To conclude this section here are some key reminders of why demonstrating the validation of your educational action research is important for teacher researchers. Based on McAteer (2020) we contend that educational action research

- is set in a real-life context, such as your classroom
- provides ways for you to generate a claim to new knowledge that is of value and therefore has an epistemological base
- is based on values such as those you have identified and studied in previous chapters. It is therefore axiologically based because axiology refers to the philosophical study of value

- dissolves the distinction between theory and practice by informing our practice through the theory we read in the literature and by generating theory from research in our practice

Conclusion

We have examined how to develop evidence of new learning from your research by establishing standards that are drawn from your values. You can check if you have met your standards by presenting your new learning to a validation group for critique. In this way you can show your research is honest and valid. The process of developing your living educational theory from researching your practice involves demonstrating that your research has had an influence in your own learning and in the learning of others and in the social formations around you. In the following chapter we will consider how your research can have an educational influence and we will look at ways of doing this.

Additional reading suggestions

Glenn, M. (2021) 'What is the educational influence of my engagement with EJOLTs (Educational Journal of Living Theories)?', *Educational Journal of Living Theories*, 14(1), 50–67, available: https://www.ejolts.net/files/373.pdf, [accessed 6 August 2022]. *Open Access.*

Kennedy, A. (2022) 'How my Living Educational Theory Research is helping me to improve my practice as a primary school teacher, in supporting children to recognise and manage their anxiety', *Educational Journal of Living Theories*, 15(2), 1–29, available: https://ejolts.net/files/Kennedy%20ejolts%2015%282%29%20393.pdf., [accessed 30 January 2023].

LaBoskey, V. (2004) 'The methodology of self-study and its theoretical underpinnings', in Loughran J.J., Hamilton M.L., LaBoskey V.K. and Russell T., eds., *International Handbook of Self-Study of Teaching and Teacher Education Practices*, Dordrecht: Kluwer, 817–870.

Smith, M.K. (2003) 'Michael Polanyi and tacit knowledge', *The encyclopedia of pedagogy and informal education* available: https://infed.org/mobi/michael-polanyi-and-tacit-knowledge/ (Webpage)

Additional resources

Delong, J. (2022) 'Dialogue as a research method', Jackie Delong in Conversation', [video], available: https://youtu.be/HUKJsYbYGtU, [accessed 28 January 2023].

Whitehead, J. (n.d.) How do I Improve What I Am Doing? Action-Reflection Planner for Improving Learning and Generating a Living-Educational-Theory, available: https://www.actionresearch.net/writings/jack/arlivingtheoryplanner.pdf., [accessed 7 August 2022].

Whitehead, J. (2022) 'Data and Standards of Judgement in Living Educational Theory', Jack Whitehead in Conversation, [video], available: https://youtu.be/vKr9LOrnFG4, [accessed 30 January 2023].

6 Generating theory and its significance

In this chapter, we will explore how to generate theory from practice and we will examine the significance of doing educational action research. One of the most exciting aspects of educational action research is that, as a practitioner researcher, you not only draw on theory to inform your thinking and enhance your practice, but you also generate theory from the process.

Key to educational action research is the idea that you consider the significance of your educational influence in your own learning, in the learning of others and in the education of social formations (Whitehead and McNiff 2006). This means that you not only develop an awareness of your influence in your own teaching, but that you are aware that you will influence others too. The others might be the children in your class or your colleagues. Once you begin to influence the policy and thinking within your community and spark interest in the thinking of others, you can say you are influencing the "education of social formations" (Whitehead 2018, p. 6). The idea of social formations is drawn from the works of philosophers such as Bourdieu (1990) and refers to a group who work together with a specific intent (McNiff and Whitehead 2011).

This chapter is organised as follows:

- the practicalities around generating theory from your research and articulating its significance
- examples of how a practising teacher generated their educational theory from practice
- why theorising practice and being aware of its potential significance is important

Section 1: Tasks to help you in generating theory from your research and in showing the possible significance of your research

Throughout your work on your project, you not only think about how you might describe your practice and your learning, but also how you might explain what happened, why it happened and what its purpose might be. Such descriptions and explanations for your new learning can lead to the creation of a living theory of your practice (Whitehead and McNiff 2006).

We are often misguided in our thinking that theory is something to be found solely in academic books on library shelves. As professional educators, and as outlined in Chapter 1,

DOI: 10.4324/9781003288183-7

we consider it our responsibility not only to read widely about educational issues and research, and thus draw on established theory, but also to generate theory from our practice (Whitehead and McNiff 2006; McAteer 2013; McDonagh *et al.* 2020) and contribute to the knowledge base of education, as outlined by Hiebert *et al.* (2002). Brydon-Miller *et al.* (2003 p. 15) remind us of the importance of that interaction between theory and practice saying that action research often goes beyond the idea that "theory can inform practice, to a recognition that theory can and should be generated through practice." They continue: "theory is really only useful insofar as it is put in the service of a practice focused on achieving positive social change." Your action research project can build a bridge between theory and practise through the action you take and the research you do in that process. As classroom researchers, we are at the heart of the action and at the heart of the research; both teacher and researcher (McDonagh *et al.* 2020).

An aspect of educational action research that practitioner researchers find stimulating is that, as a practitioner researcher, you not only draw on theory to inform your thinking and enhance your practice, but you also generate theory from the process.

You can now consider ways to:

- begin generating theory from your research
- identify your educational influence on yourself, on your own thinking and attitudes
- use your academic and professional voice to transform your learning experience and to make a real difference in the wider world of education

Ongoing tasks

Right throughout this educational action research project the interconnection between reading, dialogue, reflection and writing has been emphasised. Hopefully by now, you will see how these activities can spark new learning and help you gain new insights into your teaching and your research in practice. As you now begin to formalise your research, sharing your thinking with a validation group takes on a greater sense of importance as they either agree or disagree that your claim to new learning is accurate, fair, comprehensible and rigorously made.

You might begin the more formal writing of your research report now too. This can be initiated by taking your practice writing from earlier in the research and honing it, revising it and making it more scholarly. You can continue to read relevant literature but you can also begin to read your own writing and try to use one activity to enhance the other (McAteer 2013). By re-reading your own writing you can discover mistakes, treasures, issues of importance as well as new relationships between ideas (Feldman *et al.* 2018).

Continue to be critically reflective. Being reflexive about your practice means that you reflect on your reflective processes and observe how you see your values being lived in your practice, as outlined in Chapter 2. You should see evidence emerging to support your claim to new learning, but you should also keep a sharp eye out for any unexpected outcomes that emerge from your research. Remember that any data that shows that your practice is *not* improving or that there are few indications of living to your values is of huge relevance too. Sometimes these occasions, when there appears to be little or no data available, can become the focus of the research simply because of that lack of data (see Cassandra's research in Chapter 1). They can become opportunities for new insights and learning.

While you continue to engage critically with the literature, this might be a good opportunity to think in a more formal way about the theory/practice divide and about how you might contribute toward blurring that division. We discuss this in greater detail in Chapter 7 and we recommend some literature pertinent to this at the end of this chapter.

Tasks to help generate new theory

In the preceding chapters, we discussed the process of using theory to inform your practice through engaging professionally with the literature. Now you are going to look at how you might generate theory from your own practice. One of the basic activities that you might engage in to begin this process is to think about your new learning from undertaking your research.

Developing and progressing an answer to these questions will help you establish what your research claim might be. Once you can pin down your claim, you can begin to articulate your new theory. For example, you may have gained insight into how important the quality of interpersonal relationships within the classroom is for enhancing and extending oral language. If you can offer descriptions of this new learning and more importantly, offer explanations around this new learning, in terms of why it is important and of the purpose that it represents, then you are in the process of generating new theory (Whitehead and McNiff 2006).

Think about questions like:

Why is my new learning important?
How can I contribute to the knowledge base of the teaching profession?
What purpose does my new learning serve?
How might my new learning contribute to a more just world?

By attempting to answer these questions, you will begin to develop explanations around your new learning. Generating theory also assumes compliance with all the rigorous research processes that we have discussed in this book such as good data collection, the generation of evidence, meeting all research standards, attending to issues of ethics, rigorous validation as well as sharing and making the research account available for public scrutiny.

Tasks to help state the significance of your work

Think about the significance of your work in terms of your educational influence in your own thinking, the thinking of others and its potential significance for broader policy and practice. As teacher researchers, we have a professional responsibility to contribute to the knowledge base of our profession through generating and sharing theory (Whitehead 2021). As you draw your ideas together at the end of an action research project, the significance of your new learning for yourself and your practice will probably be quite clear. Now is the time to imagine the potential significance of your research for others. It may not be too difficult to imagine how your work might have an educational influence on your students, on other teachers in your school or colleagues in other schools. A more difficult, but worthwhile task would be to imagine your influence, or potential influence, on policy in your workplace or broader educational policy in your region or country. Whitehead (2018, p. 51) uses the term "the education of social formations" to explain this kind of influence and he perceives it as key to the process of research.

In Section 2 we show how the educational action research projects people have undertaken in their own classroom practice have had a huge influence, not only on themselves and their classroom, but also in achieving an educational influence in systemic change. It is important to be aware of the power your voice can have. You are making a contribution to the educational knowledge base and it is important to have your story heard. We will examine this in further detail in Chapter 7.

Writing tasks

The writing tasks in this chapter help you think about generating theory from your practice as you focus on the significance of your research and reflect on your previous tasks. You could start the process by writing a short piece beginning with:

> "My new learning is …" and "I will be able to demonstrate this new learning by …"
> Here you will be able to describe your new learning.

Then, try a third, and more difficult piece of writing by explaining your new learning. Begin your writing with:

> "My new learning is important because …" and "It will serve the purpose of …"
> This is only a short piece of writing but it can become draft writing for the discussion of findings section of a report. It will also be pivotal to your whole research process.

As you work through the writing task above, you should play with the ideas around the significance of the research. Begin by writing

> "I can see my educational influence in my own learning in …," "I can see my educational influence in the learning of others in …"
> and then try to address this:
> "I can see the potential of my educational influence in the education of social formations … ."

The final section is the most difficult because you have to imagine the influence your work might have on the policies and perhaps on the power-constituted relationships that impact on people's lives (Whitehead and McNiff 2006). This can become draft writing for a report conclusion section.

Validity

It is time now to begin writing about how you are addressing the validity of your research. Validation processes were discussed in detail in Chapters 4 and 5. Validity is crucial in all forms of research, but especially so when you are investigating your own practice. From the outset of the research project, you will have been taking care to embrace validity, now you need to write about it. Show, with evidence, that your story is comprehensible, truthful, sincere and appropriate for the context (Habermas 1976). Outline how you have scheduled validation meetings with critical others to establish the veracity and validity of your claim. Be sure to avoid victory narratives that only show the positive aspects of your research process. These only serve to diminish the quality and authenticity of your research.

In Figure 6.1 we have synopsised some tasks that will help to establish the significance and validity of your research:

Ongoing Tasks	Yes	No	Under Way
Continue to write a reflective journal and be reflexive	—	—	—
Continue to read and add to your draft literature review writing with a focus on the theory/practice divide and about how you might contribute toward blurring that division.	—	—	—
Continue to engage in dialogue and seek validation for your new thinking	—	—	—
Theory generation tasks			
Think about what your new learning is.	—	—	—
Think about how you might describe your new learning.	—	—	—
Think about how you might explain it.	—	—	—
Think about the significance of your work	—	—	—
Writing Tasks			
Write a short piece beginning with 'My new learning is…'.	—	—	—
Explain the significance of the research	—	—	—
Show the validity of your research claim	—	—	—

Figure 6.1 Tasks to help establish the significance of the research

Section 2: Some examples of how teachers have generated theory from practice and its educational significance

Joy Mounter is a teacher who has engaged in research in her practice and generated her living-educational-theory in that process. Her work is important for classroom researchers, because the growth in her educational influence can be traced from her own thinking about her teaching in a classroom, right up to how her research influenced educational policy in the UK.

She says:

> I have an interest in relationships in research and learning communities. I have been working on ~i~we~I~us~ as a dynamic relational value as part of my PhD research.
>
> Over many years, first as a teacher researcher, then as a headteacher researcher and now as a lecturer researcher, I researched my practice, clarified my ontological and epistemological values and gained a deeper understanding of myself in and of the world. Over the last 20 years as a Living Educational Theory Researcher, there have been two major and significant moments in my journey that have profoundly impacted my life, my thinking and my practice as a teacher. They are:
>
> 1   Finding Living Educational Theory Research (Whitehead 1989) as a way of life and continuing professional development
> 2   The second moment was as a teacher with my mixed class of 6/7/8-year-olds. I was telling them we are all learners and about my research for my Master's, when child A, asked a simple, but profound question, "How can grown-ups write about learning without us?" This changed my way of researching and writing, from ~I~ to ~we~, co-researching with my pupils
>
> The two points I have highlighted above are intrinsically intertwined and have led to the path my research is currently taking (Mounter 2019).

Initially Joy shows how she generated her values-based living-educational-theory from her practice. Her research for her master's degree asks, "As a Headteacher Researcher how can I demonstrate the impact and self-understandings drawn from Living Educational Theory Action Research, as a form of Continual Professional Development in education?" (Mounter 2012). She says:

> Working through the Action research cycle with the children as co-researchers helped me to realise the impact I have on the children in my care. This enabled me to work with the children to develop self-awareness of their talents, which they confidently articulated. At the same time I realised the impact I was having in creating a relationally, dynamic awareness of the space and boundaries we created and in which I responded continuously. This is represented in ~i~we~I~us~ as the tilde ~, often unnoticed in the educational needs of the children (Mounter 2008, p. 8). The children also created their own learning/research theory QUIFF (Question, Understanding, I am Important, Focus, Feelings), as we co-researched together, with children as co-researchers rather than purely a data set (Mounter 2012).

Joy was able to generate her living-educational-theory from her practice by offering explanations and descriptions of her learning from her values-led research. She explains:

> Having an opportunity to be a researcher in communities across my different educational roles has been very important to me personally, and for my continuing professional development. Clarifying my values as part of my Living Educational Theory Research has been a joy, as well as bringing tension into my life, as I gained a stronger awareness of my epistemological beliefs in a period of tightening Government control in education. This highlighted life-affirming energy and living contradictions (Whitehead 2018) in my practice. The energy, inspiration and feeling of being part of something bigger, something working for change and a values-led education system encouraged and renewed my commitment as an educational practitioner. My heart as an educator is drawn to both Frankl (2004) and Whitehead (2018). Frankl (1972) describes drawing a "spark" from life and Whitehead (2018, p. 1) talks about life-affirming energy "contributing to the flourishing of humanity." As a practitioner I strive to live fully my life-affirming values through my practice, making a difference in the world, creating a sense of idealism, that Frankl (2004) talks of. Through creating multiple living-educational-theories, my embodied values have become central to my life and actions, both personally and professionally (Mounter 2019).

Here we can see how clearly Joy's values inspire how she lives her life, and how she engages with her ongoing research in her practice.

She continues:

> My doctoral research is now focused on the creation and academic legitimation of my living- educational-theory-research methodology drawing from my practice as a teacher researcher, as a headteacher researcher and now as a higher education lecturer and researcher. Over the years, I have been part of different educational communities both virtual and physical. This has included various designated roles, a teacher, deputy and head teacher working in primary schools located in three English counties. My most recent work has been in helping to establish two master's programme within higher education, drawing on the principles of Living Educational Theory Research (Mounter 2021).

Joy, who is now undertaking her doctoral research, has shown clearly how her research has not only had an educational influence on herself and on her practice as head teacher, but it has also demonstrated her educational influence in her school and in her students' learning. Her passion for Living Educational Theory Research inspired her to the extent that she instigated and successfully established two MA programmes (in The Learning Institute in the UK), where the sole focus of the research is "Values-led leadership linking through Living Educational Theory Research." Her research is now of significance because she has brought her educational influence to bear in the education of social formations (Whitehead 2018), as she has clearly influenced educational policy in at least one third-level institution in the UK.

Similarly, Jim (pseudonym) is now the Headteacher of an urban post-primary school in Ireland. He began researching his own practice as an undergraduate student teacher. As you read his story ask yourself if you can see how living to his values has been at the core of Jim's educational philosophy.

In Year 4 of his undergraduate teacher education degree, Jim found himself back in the same placement school as he had been in Year 3. He says:

> It was a post-primary school and was considered to be severely disadvantaged. The student cohort was predominately drawn from children who came from broken families; from children from the traveller population; and from children whose parents were suffering from addiction or mental health problems which often meant there was consequent chaos in their lives.
>
> I was immediately struck by the fact that many of the students I had been teaching at Junior Cycle level had not returned to school for the Senior Cycle. I was very perturbed by this attrition, as I sincerely believed that education was the main path out of deprivation for those students. When I was asked to think of a research question for my final year educational action research project, I said I wanted to study "The retention of students in post-primary settings." I was reminded by my tutor, that, first of all, my research question sounded like a very propositional study, grounded in the positivist perspective of research "on" something. My tutor suggested that my research had to be "I" focused. Secondly, I only had a 12-week placement in which to conduct my study. I was advised to rethink my research focus – this time framing it as a "how can I" – type question.

Having reflected on his research question Jim returned after the weekend and said, "My question now is how can I teach in a way that does not marginalise or exclude any child?" He added, "If every teacher did that maybe the attrition question would be solved." In a conversation with his tutor, he said:

> "It would have been much easier to just do research on 'Retention in the Post-Primary sector'. A bit of reading and writing and thinking would be all that was needed and then I could go on with my life. This action research showed me that I can't just study something 'out there'. After doing even this small bit of self-study research, I see now that the buck stops here – with me. I'm 'it': I have to take responsibility for being the best teacher I can be, for being the most inclusive and just teacher I can be. It's not good enough anymore to go into the staff room and say 'I can't teach them: they don't even speak English'. I have to do something about it" (excerpt from conversation with Jim, 14 June 2013 cited in Glenn et al. 2017 pp. 117-18).

Jim worked on developing inclusive teaching strategies with four individual students. His work was grounded in strong values of social justice and fairness. After graduating, his work took him back to the same school where he taught for a number of years. His ideas were taken on board by the school and resulted in a raft of inclusive pedagogies that engaged and affirmed needy students. He organised a conference and invited students, parents, relatives, teachers, teacher educators, shopkeepers and local businesses, entrepreneurs, community liaison police officers and social workers. He invited the former governor of one of the country's largest prisons as a keynote speaker. He felt the problems that his students faced needed a community-wide response. They could not be solved by the school or parents alone.

Jim acknowledges that he always held strong values of justice and fairness and was delighted, in the final year of his undergraduate degree programme, to be afforded the opportunity to research his own practice in how he could live more faithfully to these values. His research has touched many lives and has informed his career at every stage to date. He says:

> "Looking back over my career in education to date, I have no doubt that the Educational Action Research (EAR) that I completed in Year 4 of my undergraduate degree has had the strongest influence on shaping my thinking and reflections around how I approach teaching, as well as my approach to leading and managing a school. That initial research forced me to focus on the things that I could control; in other words, to control the factors that can be controlled by me. It clicked with me that the thing that I control the most is myself; my thinking, my approach to planning, my actions, my attitude, my capacity for leadership and how I build and develop relationships with others. The most common questions that I ask myself now always start with 'how can I ... .?' Asking questions in this way automatically focuses on a mindset that aims to improve my practice and is solution-focused, which I hope will improve the experiences and outcomes for others [students, staff and parents/ guardians]. I also regularly use the work of Stephen Brookfield to inform my reflections when I facilitate consultations with the school community that I lead. In my opinion, EAR is rooted in Dewey's work about knowledge being socially constructed based on experiences. Education can often be ambiguous and is rarely black and white. EAR allows me to operate in that area of ambiguity and work to make the best decisions and choices within the context in which I work." (email conversation with J. 20 May 2022)

Jim's educational values are still to the fore of his life and his work. With reflection and further study, they have been honed and developed further, but the foundations remain firm ever since his first foray into educational action research in college, over a decade ago.

Now we will explain why generating theory from practice is important and we will outline why being aware of the significance of your research is part of the research process itself.

Section 3: Contributing to educational knowledge and transformation

Your own lived experiences are key in generating your living educational theory. Your theory goes beyond describing what has happened in your research and what you have learned.

It also requires making your explanations of what has happened in your research public in order to show their veracity. Now we will focus on another aspect of developing your theory – its significance. This means you will show your "influence in your own learning, in the learning of others and in the learning of the social formations within which the practice is located" (Whitehead 2018, p. 113) which we will now discuss.

By now you will probably have realised that many significant changes have happened because of your research. As you reflect critically on them, the importance of your research will become clearer to you. In this section we explain the various ways in which your research can contribute to new educational knowledge and why this is important. This will reveal the new perspectives that have developed from your research, as well as the power of generating theory from your research for yourself, your profession and your co-researchers. It will show the significance of changing attitudes and of making a difference, not only in your practice but also in the real world around you. We look next at the significance of conducting educational action research on your practice under the following headings.

- new practices and perspectives that have developed
- its educational influence
- the transformative power of your research for sustainable professional development
- the relevance of developing a professional and academic voice

The importance of the new practices and perspectives developed from your research

You began your research with a view to enhancing your practice. When you analyse your data, new ideas and evidence about improvements in your professional practice emerge. These new ideas may still be emerging because learning about practice is an ongoing process. Teacher researchers recognise that it is well worth the effort and commitment required, in terms of the benefits ensuing both for you and your students. Without you and your research, these new professional practices would not have emerged. We suggest that you look over the new learning in your research again and ask yourself why is this important to you as a person, as a teacher and as a researcher.

Educational action research is often about developing a better understanding of oneself. Carozzi (2019), for example, tells how her research into her practice as a development manager grew through the writing-up process. By enquiring into what exactly her practice was, engaging actively with the literature and recognising the importance of dialectic relationships, she realised that her practice was not to develop others. Instead, it was to understand herself better. She describes this as "a question of self-definition and self-identification; selfhood and self-realization" (p. 53). Her writing became an ongoing self-questioning and self-individualising process in which she linked "actions, words, meanings and thoughts" (Carozzi 2019, p. 53). Therefore, her learning from research led to new deep ontological perspectives.

New perspectives can emerge through relational learning that may develop during your research, as in the following example. Gumede undertook research in his role as a black

African (Zulu) male educator who became a head teacher of a rural high school. "My research has taught me humility in accepting that I need to be relearning a new way of learning and listening" (Gumede 2020, p. 2). He attributes his new perspectives not to himself as an individual but as a participant in a collective endeavour. His research enabled him to comprehend his values of ubuntu (humanity) and inhlonipho (respect) more fully. He discerned the importance of his ideas with the historical and current insights on leadership as well as the limited resources in his setting. The South African Proverb – *Umuntu umuntu ngabantu* (people are people because of other people) encompassed his new understandings and his awareness of learning and listening together as key elements in his leadership

In both of these instances the researchers gained new perspectives because of conducting what may have initially seemed a practical study of their practice. While their research generated changes in these practices, it also validated new theories for the researchers.

In your research you will demonstrate that you have tried to fulfil your values. You will have evidence to support your claim to have created new knowledge (as outlined in Chapter 5). Your claim to knowledge, which arises from your new learning around your educational practice, represents your personal theory of your practice, or your living educational theory (Whitehead 2018).

Your research potentially has an educational influence

We use the term *educational influence* to show that your new learning, from the theory you have generated from your practice, has some real influence and is not just about taking action for practical change. Its impact can influence yourself and others outside your research. Whitehead explains the term educational as "learning with a life-affirming energy and values that carry hope for the flourishing of humanity" (Whitehead 2018, p. 92). Glenn (2021, p. 54) says such research "has created an environment that enhances learning and stimulates people, including myself, to take responsibility for our own learning." While you are conducting your research, you may have already shown that you have influenced your own learning and the learning of participants. This includes those participants who observed and critiqued your research. Once your formal period of research is complete, you begin to share it publicly, which we describe in Chapter 7. This adds another layer of significance to the educational implications of your work.

To establish their educational influence, many teacher researchers examine the relevance of their research for all its participants – students, teachers, school community. Looking for examples of where you have influenced the wider education community's knowledge and practice can be an empowering experience. This educational influence is about people coming together to establish collaborative practices so as "to share our knowledge, disseminate our ideas and encourage others to do the same" (McDonagh *et al.* 2020, p. 116).

Like us authors, many researchers find that educational action research becomes not only a research approach, but also an approach to teaching and, often, it even becomes a way of life. Griffin and Delong (2021) explain this well. In their paper the two authors, who are practitioner researchers, collaboratively share the ways in which Living Educational Theory has helped them to improve their practice and transform their lives. They describe and explain the influence of their research in their learning, in the learning of others and in social formations, and then tell how their research process became a "way of living/life" (p. 26). They also highlight that the sustainability of their research approach lies in the recognition of the educational influence of the research.

In summary the educational influence of your research demonstrates that you have engaged in a sustainable and credible form of research where you have taken responsibility for your own learning and shared your new knowledge with others.

The transformative power of your research for sustainable professional development

At its simplest, theory means an idea. In research, theories in education are often about understanding how people learn and theory is a way to explain, describe, analyse and predict learning. As teacher researchers we are examining how we teach in order to support such learning. Living Theory (Whitehead and McNiff 2006) provides a theoretical framework or structure which explains how we may generate theory from our educational action research study into our practice. Many teacher researchers have found that their living theories have challenged and extended existing knowledge and assumptions which can lead to transformation.

By conducting your educational action research, you can transform both your thinking and your practice. Transformation lies at the heart of all educational action research. Kemmis *et al.* (2014, p. 65) use the term "practice architectures" to describe how practices are held in place. They suggest that changing a practice requires "not only changing the sayings, doings, relatings and the project that constitute the practice" but also the "practice architectures – the cultural-discursive, material-economic and social-political arrangements – that hold the practice in place." Change needs to take place at many levels for transformation to be sustainable.

We will now explain this process by using three examples (i) Wood (2010), (ii) Rahmann *et al.* (2021) and (iii) Gonzalez *et al.* (2021). Each of these generated their own living-educational-theories. The significance of the living-educational-theories of these and many other living theorists is that they transformed their practice as a form of sustainable professional development as they blurred the boundaries between theory and practice. This, along with other similar research findings, has convinced us of the significance of this research approach for continuing professional learning.

i Wood (2010) explains a project that she undertook with teachers from disadvantaged schools in South Africa. The significance of its transformative effect was that the teachers changed their practice as they created their insider epistemologies and practices for HIV prevention. Wood helped them to see their potential as agents of change. She claims that change begins with oneself, and her transformation occurred as she learned to live her values of mutual respect and sincerity more fully in her institution. Her work has influenced colleagues in her practice too as they adopted self-study action research in their practice as a strategy to enhance teaching (Wood 2010).

ii Rahmann *et al.* (2021) tell of the transformative potential of the research methodology. They developed a "transformative, cooperative living-educational-theory" (p. 26) with children and youth in the Education for Development and Sustainability Community of Practice (EDFCP) in Bangladesh. Their initial question was "How can we explain the related inner change?" (p. 26) as they mentored vulnerable children and youth to become change agents, teachers and leaders who, in turn, mentor younger children and youth. They realised that the motivation for a change in identity must be "deeply rooted in the learner to justify the effort needed for transformation" (p. 37). They showed that transformation is "triggered by a disorienting dilemma," or living contradiction as we have described it earlier in this book. This is the very process you are engaging in with your research approach. As a teacher researcher you examine, question and revise assumptions, beliefs and values assimilated uncritically from your own culture and community, and discover your own values, purpose and meanings. The validation processes of your theory of practice are also significant because as Rahmann *et al.* (2021 p. 31) suggest, transformation is an emotional and holistic process which includes "relational and emotional ways of knowing."

iii Gonzales *et al.* (2021) write about how living-theory transforms teacher education for them. As Americans working with Masters' students in the Bahamas, they questioned, "How is my/our professional learning impacted as we collaboratively construct curricular experiences for fellow educators in an international context, which focused on the social, cultural, and historical context of our actions in this professional learning relationship?" (p. 1). As they encouraged student researchers to transform within their own practices, they discovered that it was a democratising process which developed "new knowledge production for teachers and learners who have been historically marginalised" (Gonzales *et al.* 2021, p. 21).

The relevance of developing a professional and academic voice

Having opportunities to develop their professional voice is important in the lives of teachers and should be a feature of their practice from the beginning of their career. Kalmbach Phillips and Carr (2014) highlight how the process of learning and doing action research enables preservice teachers to grow a strong and trustworthy professional voice to engage students, parents and colleagues in critical conversation for change. Similarly, in an ever-growing culture that deprofessionalises teachers by reducing the academic standards for teacher qualification (Ravitch 2022) and promotes scripted curricula and teacher-proof materials (Fitz and Nikolaidis 2020), having the voice of the teacher heard has never been as important.

A major importance of developing your living educational theory, therefore, is that it enables you to speak in an authoritative voice. This process begins from the moment you start to make your research public, by opening it up to others such as your critical friends and validation group. Kalmbach Phillips and Carr (2014) remind us that by conducting your research:

> ... you will become a teacher more equipped to thrive in a professional environment where sometimes teachers may be undervalued, underpowered, and at times even silenced by the culture of schooling.
>
> (Kalmbach Phillips and Carr 2014, p. 2)

When you have created your theory of practice, you have greater confidence in what you have learned and you have found your voice. You may begin to use your voice to counter the hegemony that posits the proposition that teachers themselves don't really matter and "can be replaced by strict instructions, behavioural performance, standards for output and quality control" (Kelchtermans 2009, p. 258).

We recall Schön's (1995) topography of the swampy lowlands of practitioner research. Schön (1995) described how practitioners occupied the swampy lowlands of practice while theorists dwelt in a lofty high ground that may have little bearing on the reality of the lives of the practitioners. Traditionally, teachers have lived in the swampy lowlands (Schön 1995). There we toiled daily in our classrooms, staring upwards and outwards towards others who defined the knowledge base. These included theorists from sociology, psychology, psychiatry, well-being and behaviour management as well as curriculum developers and major policymakers. Teachers were perceived as implementers of policy and of working at the level of practitioner only. Their voices remained "largely silent" (Oancea 2014, p. 514) and their work was mainly curtailed to the practical implementation of their guidelines.

Gradually, and in more recent times, generating one's living educational theory from one's practice has helped to change these perceptions. It has helped to enable teacher voice and generate respect for teacher professional knowledge. You now have an authoritative voice on research and theory generation, and you can explain why this is so. You are beyond the swampy lowlands (Schön 1995) and your research has added to the knowledge base of the profession. Sadly many teachers still conduct evaluation and research on their practice and do not have the expertise to raise this to a theoretical level as you have learned to do in this book. Teachers who continue to conduct valid educational action research have the potential to become leaders both in professional learning as well as in policy-making contexts.

Conclusion

In this chapter, you have investigated ways in which you might generate theory from your research process. You have explored how you might explain the development of your living-educational-theory in terms of descriptions of what happened, and explanations around why it happened and what its purpose might be. This brought you to explicitly stating the potential significance of your research.

Kalmbach Phillips and Carr (2014) remind us that living theory "is the deliberate act of pausing to think through what we know, how we know it, and alternative ways to frame our knowing" (p. 128). In the next chapter we learn how to explore different ways of making this new knowledge and theory public.

Additional reading suggestions

Schön, D.A. (1995) 'Knowing-in-action: The new scholarship requires a new epistemology', *Change (New Rochelle, N.Y.)*, 27(6), 27–34, available: 10.1080/00091383.1995.10544673

Mavhunga, E. and Merwe, D. V.D. (2020) 'Bridging science education's theory-practice divide: A perspective from teacher education through topic-specific PCK', *African Journal of Research in Mathematics, Science and Technology Education*, 24(1), 65–80, available: 10.1080/18117295.2020.1716496

Sachs J. (2016) 'Teacher professionalism: why are we still talking about it?', Teachers and Teaching, Theory and Practice, 22(4), 413–425, available: 10.1080/13540602.2015.1082732.

Suggested resources

Delong J. (2022) 'Living Educational Theory as a Way of Life' *Jackie Delong in Conversation*, [video], available: https://youtu.be/hYgIPGxtZ78, [accessed 30 January 2023].

Whitehead J. (2022) 'What is Living Educational Theory?', *Jack Whitehead in Conversation*, [video], available: https://youtu.be/YsmFLTBdPGg, [accessed 30 January 2023].

7 Writing up and disseminating: Sharing the story of your learning

In this chapter, you will be introduced to the processes involved in writing an account of your research, as well as being offered some guidance around how to disseminate what you learned. Going public with your research began when you looked for critique from friends and validation groups. Teacher researchers can share their research with participants and colleagues in a variety of ways. These might include presentations to parents and pupils; to staff colleagues; at staff meetings; to teachmeets; in professional magazines, e-zines; in podcasts and webinars; to teacher conferences and research networks. In addition to sharing your research in order to receive feedback and questions so as to develop your ideas, there are two further reasons for going public – accreditation requirements and expanding the influence of your research. In this chapter we will comment on each, beginning with writing a formal research report.

The chapter explores

- the practicalities of writing and disseminating a research account
- the significance of writing and sharing research accounts, from those who have already done this
- why writing and sharing the research story is of the utmost importance in the research process

Section 1: How do I write an account of my research and share it?

You have been writing continuously throughout, but now, you are embarking on the preparation of your actual research report. This is a different or more formal kind of writing. A formal report may be a requirement of an accredited programme, or may be required by a bursary awarding group, or even for a school board of management or school head. You may feel that this kind of writing is less attractive to you. You are not alone: Herr and Anderson (2015) are of the opinion that action researchers are frequently more interested in doing the research than in writing it up!

This is understandable when we consider that practitioner researchers are focused on the action, on doing something to enhance their practice. However, if you want to show your educational influence in your "own learning and life, the learning and lives of others, and the social formations within which we [you] live" (Whitehead 2018, pp. 1-2) it generally becomes

DOI: 10.4324/9781003288183-8

necessary to produce a written report of the research. Herr and Anderson (2015) concur with this view:

> A dissertation forces action researchers to think not only about what knowledge they have generated that can be fed back into the setting (local knowledge), but also what knowledge they have generated that is transferable to other settings (public knowledge).
>
> Herr and Anderson (2015, p. 10)

Dissemination is a critical part of the research process. In fact, McNiff (2002, np) suggests that when you come to write your report or seek to make your research public in other ways, you should aim to show:

> ... not only the actions of your research, but also the learning involved. Some researchers focus only on the actions and procedures, and this can weaken the authenticity of the research.
>
> (McNiff 2002, np)

In this section we begin looking at the different stages involved in writing an account of your research. Whitehead and McNiff (2006) attest to the fact that doing your research and writing a text about it are two different activities requiring two different sets of skills: doing your research is a social activity whereas writing about it is mainly an individual practice. They go on to explain that

> Writing action research accounts involves two things: it involves writing in a way that communicates the processes of the research, and it also involves writing in a way that maintains the reader's attention throughout and speaks to their own experiences.
>
> (Whitehead and McNiff 2006, p. 140)

The challenge, then, is to create a text that is of scholarly quality while being accessible to your readers.

Remember that there are various stages to writing: planning, free-writing, writing drafts, revising, editing. Readers need a route map to guide them through the report, so be sure to write a good introduction to make it clear to your readers what they are about to read. This may be the first draft of your introduction. Synopsising your research for the introduction will help you to focus clearly on what needs to go into your account. However, some writers prefer to write the introduction after the research report is complete.

You have already engaged in a lot of informal writing, for example when you undertook any of the writing tasks that we suggested in previous chapters. You may also have had some writing practice when you recorded events in your reflective journal, when you noted the details of your data collection and when you produced a draft of your literature review. Now that you are about to write a report on the whole process of engaging in your research, you will need to adopt a more formal structure for your writing, particularly if your research was undertaken for academic purposes. The practice writing that you have produced prior to this will certainly be of benefit to you as you hone your writing skills in order to create the best possible account of your research. We will provide guidelines for you as you undertake this task, under the following headings:

- a possible structure for your research report
- the importance of using an appropriate writing style
- ensuring that you have a sense of your readership
- the necessity to draft and redraft your writing
- sharing the story of your research with others

Structuring your research report

When you come to the stage of writing an account of your research, there are certain elements that should be included, particularly if you are writing as part of an accredited programme. As with most pieces of writing, whether a short essay or a longer document, you will need an introduction and conclusion. In between, there can be a variety of chapters, depending on your readership and the purpose of your written account. If you are writing a report on your research mainly for your own benefit, or to make a presentation to colleagues or at a conference, you could use headings such as Research Title, Overview of Research, Rationale and Aims, Research Topic, Design and Methodology, Findings and Recommendations. If, on the other hand, you are writing for accreditation purposes or for an academic journal, and if you have not been provided with any specific guidance around the structure of the document, we suggest the following format as a possible structure (Figure 7.1) for your writing:

- Front Matter
- Abstract
- Introduction
- Chapter One: Background
- Chapter Two: Literature Review
- Chapter Three: Methodology
- Chapter Four: Data Analysis
- Chapter Five: Findings and discussion of findings
- Chapter Six: The significance of your research
- Conclusion
- References
- Appendices (if required)

Figure 7.1 Layout of a formal research report

Looking at the above layout for a research report or dissertation, its neat and formal linearity is in stark contrast to the real-life experience of engaging in an action research project. The action part involves a cyclical process of plan, act, observe and reflect (Kemmis and McTaggart 2000). This does not fit easily into a beginning-middle-end form of representation. Many practitioner researchers describe their research experience as involving various twists and turns along the way (Mellor 2001; Cook 2009) which makes it difficult to present their research in a neat problem-free package with no loose ends. Some researchers can feel discouraged by their experience of the messiness and unwieldiness of their research. However, Brydon-Miller *et al.* (2003) suggest that we should be tolerant and accepting of such conflicts and uncertainties. They describe these messes as the beauty of chaos in order to illustrate the fact that action researchers are accustomed to engaging constantly with complex problems as they seek to bring about improvement in their situation. Nevertheless, practitioner researchers may find it a challenge to fit their research into a framework that was developed for more traditional forms of research. Some educational institutions will allow students to deviate from the traditional format in favour of more creative reporting methods such as the inclusion of videos as data sources. However, this brings its own challenges. For example, you would need to show that using videos does not contravene data protection guidelines and does not compromise your ethical commitments to your participants.

In our description of how to write your research report, we will use a traditional format for writing dissertations, as this is acceptable to most academic institutions. It would be important for those submitting their research for academic accreditation to follow closely the guidelines of their institution in this matter. Bear in mind that you may have to adhere to a word count. A strict formatting style may be required also, for example, a particular font, margin width, specific spacing and perhaps justified text. These will all be clearly communicated to you in advance. However, we encourage you to be as creative as possible in reporting your research within the confines of the procedures requested by your institution. We will now give you suggestions as to what you might include in each chapter as outlined in the table above. Feel free to modify this for your own needs.

Front Matter

Here you will provide a title page, a table of contents; a list of figures or tables – if necessary; a list of appendices – if appropriate; a list of abbreviations or acronyms; and your acknowledgements.

Abstract

This is a brief overview of your research. It should include the research question and the main findings. Generally this is written last, after you have completed the full report. It usually has a strict word count and may require particular formatting, such as single-spaced and in italics.

Introduction: What is my concern?

This is an opportunity for you to tell your readers a little bit about yourself, your context and about your chosen research topic. You might explain who or what inspired you to undertake your research. You could regard this as the space where you set the scene for the chapters to follow, giving a brief account of what the reader may expect to find in each chapter. It can be an opportunity for engaging the attention of your readers. You might address the question "What is my concern?"

Chapter One: Background: Why am I concerned?

In this chapter you could provide the background for your research and the context within which your research took place. You could give the rationale for your research by explaining what you wanted to do and why you wanted to do it. This is where you answer the question "Why am I concerned?" Your educational values will need to be to the fore in these explanations. A few details about your own educational situation would also be helpful and perhaps you could indicate what is most important to you in the field of education. A knowledge of the concepts underpinning your educational stance will help your readers to understand your research process and the trajectory it takes.

Chapter Two: Literature review: Looking through the lens of educational theory

The literature review chapter is an opportunity for you to demonstrate the range of literature you have managed to access. It would be important to include literature pertaining to your chosen research methodology so that your readers will understand this approach. Discussing the relevant literature is vital but this must not be at a descriptive level only. You need to critically engage with the ideas in the literature and justify why you agree or do not agree with the ideas. Bear in mind also that your use of the literature is not confined to this chapter – it needs to permeate the whole document and so you should cite theories from the literature throughout your report whenever there is an opportunity to do so. This chapter is about showing the reader of your report how you went about understanding the area you are studying. In traditional research it was generally written before the research took place. As action research is an approach that is about ongoing action, learning and evaluating, and because the literature is woven throughout the report, a stand-alone literature review chapter is not an absolute necessity (Coghlan 2022).

Chapter Three: Methodology: What did I plan to do, and how?

There are a few different elements that need attention in the methodology chapter. You need to discuss your educational action research approach and explain why it is appropriate for your research. You need to highlight that a distinctive aspect of this study is the focus on your practice and the use of "I" throughout. You can say who your participants are and why they were chosen. Ethical issues can be highlighted in this chapter, and you could describe the steps you have taken to ensure good ethical practice, such as receiving permission to undertake the research, getting consent and assent forms signed, promising confidentiality and anonymity, and allowing right of withdrawal. An outline of your research plan and the timeframe for implementing it can be included here. You can provide a summary of your data collection tools and the purpose of each one. If you intend to have critical friends and a validation group for the purpose of triangulation of your data, it would be good to mention it in this chapter. Your values should be a key feature here as you will use them to describe the standards by which you wish your research to be assessed.

Chapter Four: Data analysis: What did I find out?

The data analysis chapter will require a high level of concentration as you focus on the various pieces of data that you have collected and as you try to match them to the aims of your research, to your research question and to your values. Your reflective journal and the feedback from your students will help with this process. You will also have the feedback from your critical friend and from your validation group. With all of these sources of evidence, you should have a strong case for making your claim to new knowledge about your educational practice.

Chapter Five: Findings and discussion: My new learning

Now that you have identified your findings through analysing your data thoroughly, it would be good to examine them in greater detail and to draw conclusions from them. You could, for instance, look at what effect, positive or negative, the research findings have had on your practice. You could also discuss the educational influence you have had in the lives of your students and colleagues through involving them in your research. It would be good to keep an open mind as you look at your findings, as there may be unexpected or unplanned findings, and these can be just as valid and influential as your anticipated findings.

Chapter Six: The significance of your research: The "So what" factor

At this point in your report, you discuss the significance that your research has had for you at a personal, professional and theoretical level. If you wish to discuss this significance or the theoretical aspects of your research in your findings chapter, that is acceptable also. Tell the readers what your new learning is. Show how you have generated a theory from your practice in terms of offering descriptions of your learning and giving explanations of how this happened and its purpose (McNiff 2010). However, you may prefer to devote a separate chapter to your living educational theory. This is where you outline how your theory developed from your engagement in research in your practice. You could clarify the role of your values in the development of your theory. Expanding on your theory of practice in this manner will add to its significance and will contribute to meeting the requirements for an academic qualification.

Conclusion: Where next?

Besides drawing together all the elements of your research in the conclusion, you could mention any plans you have for continuing on with your research. This idea could appeal to you if your experience of carrying out your research has been a positive one and has benefited both you and your students. You may feel that continuing to live to your values may have long-term effects on your educational practice. You could also consider possibilities for sharing your research with colleagues and for disseminating your research to a wider audience. We will discuss possibilities for achieving this further on in this chapter.

References/Bibliography

Throughout your research report, you will have cited numerous authors. These need to be included in a references section at the end of your report. The names of the authors are listed in alphabetical order and other details are also required, such as the year of publication for a book, journal article or paper; the title of the book, journal article or paper; for a book, the place of publication and the publishing company; for a journal article, the number of the issue and the relevant page numbers; for a paper, the details of the conference at which it was presented. It would be good practice to note the details of any citations as you use them as this will make it easier for you to compile your list of references, as mentioned in Chapter 6.

Appendices

It is not necessary to include appendices, but it can prove useful to do so. You may, for example, find that you have exceeded the recommended word count in the main text of your report, in which case you may be able to transfer some items to an appendix. Among the items that you could transfer are pieces of data such as standardised or teacher-designed test results, transcripts of taped discussions or interviews and feedback from students and critical friends. You could discuss these pieces of data in the main text and refer your reader to the relevant appendix for the full account.

The importance of using an appropriate writing style

People write research reports for many reasons, as we show in Section 2 of this chapter. We begin by discussing academic writing which refers to the standard of writing acceptable to accrediting institutions. Some teacher researchers, for example, those who receive bursaries, are expected to write a report of academic standard to complete the bursary process. Some research reports are designed for specific audiences and may not necessarily be written or presented in an academic style of writing. We will look at these in more detail under the next heading of ensuring that you have a sense of your readership.

This section will be particularly relevant to you if you are carrying out your research for accreditation purposes. If you would like to submit your research account for publication in an educational journal at some stage, it would be to your advantage to begin using an academic style of writing. The language used in academic writing is more formal than your everyday speech. The use of contractions, therefore, would be inappropriate and so, for example, you should use the format "do not" and "cannot," rather than "don't" and "can't." The style of writing needs to be focused and specific. The content should be easily understood by the reader and so you should avoid any sentence structures that appear complex or complicated. Clarity is an important feature of the writing process and can ensure that your ideas are intelligible to readers of your research.

There is a view shared by many in academia that academic writing should be objective, that it should be written in the third person and that the writer's opinion should not feature in the writing. However, in many forms of action research, including our form of educational action research, you are researching your own "I" as you endeavour to enhance your practice through living to your values. Consequently, your own opinion is of the utmost importance. The proponents of the objectivist stance may claim that their approach eliminates bias on the part of the researcher. Bias can also be reduced in the case of first-person research using corroborative feedback from participants which can contribute to the validation of your personal interpretations and findings of your research.

Having a sense of your readership

As you engage with the writing of your report, put yourself in the place of the listener or reader to see if the content makes sense to you and if there is a logical sequence to your arguments. If you are having difficulty in understanding any aspect of your report, you might need to engage in further explanations in order to ensure clarity around your ideas. You could ask a friend or colleague to read your report with a critical eye and their feedback could be invaluable in identifying areas that might need clarification. This action could be especially useful if you are undertaking your research for academic accreditation or if you hope to publish your research.

Some teacher researchers present progress and complete research reports to peers during accredited courses. Others may present to participants, be they pupils or their parents, during and after their research actions. The reasons they do this may be to get feedback, to get validation or to comply with their ethical requirements to keep participants informed in case they may wish to withdraw from the research. Being aware of those who are listening to, or reading, your research will determine how you will present it. In Section 2 of this chapter, you will see how the use of video, anecdotes and virtual resources helped show a sense of listener/reader awareness.

The drafting processes

Anyone who has produced an academic piece of writing is aware of the necessity to draft and redraft the work. The first attempt will contain your fledgling ideas, possibly described in basic and simple language. As you develop your ideas through your engagement with the literature and discussions with colleagues, you will begin to frame them in a more scholarly manner. Each time you read over your work, you will try to find a better and clearer way of expressing your ideas. As we mentioned in the previous paragraph, asking a friend or colleague to read a draft with a critical eye could result in a more focused and erudite piece of writing. It could also help to eradicate any errors, both in syntax and in referencing, that you may have overlooked. Continuous drafting will ensure that your research account is as error-free as possible and is of good quality. Of course, at some point you will have to come to a decision that you have refined your piece of writing as much as you can and that it is now time to submit it. This decision may be made for you if you are submitting to an academic institution.

Making time for writing, drafting and redrafting can pose a challenge for many teacher researchers who are not full-time students. The approaches to getting a research report written are as individual as the teacher/researchers themselves. Some may meet this challenge by making a long-term writing and drafting plan and following it assiduously. Others may choose to build up the report gradually by doing a little writing daily. We have found it useful to recognise things that distract us from writing and to actively avoid them if possible! If you are spending some hours on the writing process, try to schedule breaks.

Here are a few strategies some busy teachers/researchers have tried. Some attempt to chunk the tasks, spend a specific but short time on one and move on to the next chunk; then after a time revisit the script. Others try listing the headings in the structure or framework of their report. They work to these but not necessarily in order. Another approach is not to stop writing at the end of a section but to continue and write just one or two sentences of the next section and then stop. This enables the writer to pick up ideas and thoughts from where they left off when they next have time to continue writing.

Sharing your research with others

Once you have written up your research report, you should begin to think about how your finished work should be disseminated. As outlined in previous chapters, sharing the theory you have generated is important for you, as well as adding to the knowledge base for other education students and teachers.

If your research has been carried out for the purpose of accreditation, you will submit it to the relevant academic institution. This will provide it with a professional but limited readership. However, whether your research is undertaken for academic purposes or simply for your own desire to enhance your practice, there are options for the wider dissemination of your research. You might, for example, consider publishing an article in the journal attached to your Union or professional body. Student Teacher Educational Research (STER) is an Irish Higher Education partnership project that supports education students to share their dissertation research with the wider education community. Their e-journal is available at https://www.ster.ie/journal.html.

Depending on the focus of your research, you might opt to submit a paper to a journal with your subject specialism. Taking Literacy as an example, there are several to choose from: *The Reading Teacher*; *The Journal of Literacy Research*; *Journal of Research in Reading* and many more. Literacy Associations internationally are likely to have their own journals.

You might share your research with other practitioners in your field by volunteering to present your work-in-progress or finished work to your colleagues as part of in-house continuous professional development (CPD). You could also inform your local education centre about your work and volunteer to present at an evening professional development session.

If you are engaged in an accredited course, you may get the opportunity to present your work to fellow students or you may wish to submit an overview of your work in the form of an academic paper to a peer-refereed journal. Again, there are many of these and we have included a suggested list at the end of this chapter. Some journals offer writers proactive support from reviewers to ensure papers meet publishable criteria. Whichever publication route you choose, you may need to adapt your report to suit the readership of the journal. It might be an option to publish part of your research, or to abstract a particular vignette from it, that you feel could be of interest to other educators. The journal you choose will probably have guidelines to help you in making decisions in this regard.

In this section, we have examined how we might write and disseminate an educational action research report or account. We have synopsised the steps you might undertake in this process in Figure 7.2.

Writing Up Tasks	**Yes**	**No**	**Under way**
Use the draft writing you have already produced to begin the formal writing up of your project. Remember you are telling the story of your learning in terms of enhancing practice and living in the direction of your values.	—	—	—
Select the appropriate headings/format for your report	—	—	—
Check the tone of your writing suits the report (formal, academic or casual)	—	—	—
Check that referencing is in place and accurate	—	—	—

Sharing your research	**Yes**	**No**	**Under Way**
You have been sharing your draft work with critical friends and at validation sessions. Now that you have tcompleted this phase of your research, you can share your claim to knowledge with colleagues in your school or in a local education centre.	—	—	—
Decide whether you want to share your research formally in an academic setting or in a more informal setting.	—	—	—

Figure 7.2 Writing up and disseminating: Sharing the story of your learning

Section 2: Writing and sharing: Stories from practitioner researchers

In this section, we will demonstrate how others have successfully written up and disseminated their educational action research projects. Sharing the account of your research can begin informally and move on quickly to formal dissemination. This process can be transformational at both a personal and a professional level. Sharing your account and receiving constructive feedback can lead you to being more confident about your work. This confidence can stem from being able to provide evidence that shows that what you are doing matters, and much of it comes from having reflected critically on your practice. Brookfield (2017) explains how, having critically examined our practice, we are better equipped to provide a rationale for why we do what we do. The critically reflective habit, he says "confers a deeper benefit than that of procedural utility. It grounds not only our actions but also our sense of who we are as teachers in an examined reality; we know why we believe what we believe" (p. 81).

We begin with the story of the authors of this book as they began to write and disseminate their research collaboratively. The second example is from Mary as she shows how she moved from teacher researcher to educational influencer.

The authors' story of writing collaboratively

All four of us authors can now look back with some bemusement at how our lives, collectively and individually, were completely changed by the dissemination of our research.

We began by sharing our work-in-progress, as teachers researching our individual practice, at a specially convened action research conference in our university. We requested and got both written and oral feedback on our presentations. As expected, some was positive, which was affirming and lovely; some was negative, which, naturally, didn't feel so lovely. Reflecting critically on the feedback, we began to unpack why we felt the way we did; what we could learn about our own identity as teachers; what, if necessary, might be changed. We went on to present together and individually at seminars, colloquia, national and international conferences and continuous professional development meetings.

We formed a writing group and co-authored and published several books and papers together. These were written by teachers for teachers. We reflected critically on all feedback as we made our research public, and this led us to write about a research process to enhance practice in (McDonagh et al. 2012 and 2020), developing educational learning partnerships through action research in (Glenn et al. 2017) critical reflection and action research (Sullivan et al. 2016) the dialectical relationship that exists between theory and practice in the current climate of accountability (Glenn 2016).

We are referring to our collaborative writing because we believe that writing a good quality research report is not only about putting your research pieces like a jigsaw into a research report framework. It requires skills such as organising ideas; being practical especially about time constraints; staying on track; being reflective; presenting logical arguments; reading widely; being a storyteller; being imaginative; showing how you are constantly questioning; strongly stating your reasons for acting and researching; communicating with and engaging your reader; keeping the big picture in mind so that the reader can easily understand your work.

We were teacher researchers in primary schools, and as we wrote about our research, we began to have some influence in other educational sectors, nationally and internationally. We recognised that teacher researchers did not have as many opportunities to write about their classroom research as did students engaged in accredited programmes.

We wanted to provide a platform for practitioner researchers to have their voices heard. Consequently we expanded our research actions and reported on them in virtual environments as follows:

We formed an association called EARI – Educational Action Research Ireland – and subsequently NEARI – the Network for Educational Action Research of Ireland. We hold three conferences/meetings per year, see http://www.eari.ie/neari-network-for-educational-action-research-in-ireland/

We have also formed a special interest group (SIG) the Educational Studies Association of Ireland (ESAI) - see Values-based Practitioner Action Research http://esai.ie/sigs-2020/

A key learning from this example is how collaboration in the writing process can help to clarify one's thinking and develop a greater confidence. It becomes a dialogue in and on writing. These research conversations pointed us towards both identifying the importance of disseminating our research and also finding ways to disseminate it. Next, in Mary's story she tells her individual story of sharing her research.

Mary's experiences of sharing her work

During her classroom research studies, with a class group of 8-9-year-olds, Mary Roche tells how she began her writing process. She aimed to research dialogical pedagogies that would support children to be critical thinkers. Picturebooks and dialogue were among the tools she used as she encouraged critical thinking and book talk. Here is how Mary's dissemination writing began.

After every three or four weeks of data gathering, I would type out transcripts of our classroom picturebook discussions and give them to the children to read. This led to a lot of new insights for me (See Roche 2007). With more junior classes, where the children were too young to read for themselves, I read the scripts aloud, and I gave copies of transcripts to their parents. The feedback led to a lot of new learning for me. With the permission of the school authorities, I also invited parents to attend some after-school sessions, where I showed videos of classroom discussions. The feedback from those was invaluable and showed me how children were often continuing our discussions at home.

Mary was expected by the School Head to induct new teachers to the Critical Thinking and Book Talk process. Conversations developed.

I did this by scheduling in-class continuous professional development whereby teachers were released from duty to sit in on classroom discussions and to be mentored, if needed, on holding their own discussions with their own classes. All of this formal and informal dissemination was beneficial for me: it consolidated my own emerging personal educational theory; it provided me with lots of data for considera-tion; it led to new learning for myself and others; it had a positive influence in the pedagogical relationships with my students, and in relationships with their parents. It opened up all kinds of researcherly "professional conversations" with colleagues. (Clark 2001, p. 172)

Mary explains that her journey to dissemination as largely grounded in "hunches and happenstance" (McDonagh *et al.* 2020, p. 34). She shared anecdotes from her research with other schools and classrooms. Occasionally, people said she should put these into a book but, at the time, she didn't feel confident enough to present her work formally with others. However, she did a talk about her learning at in-house staff CPD days. When she was invited by a local Education Centre to provide a summer course for teachers, many doors opened, and she was asked to present her work at research conferences. Mary tells of how her writing progressed as follows:

> I submitted a paper to InTouch (Roche 2001a); The Journal for the Association of Teachers of Philosophy for Children (Roche 2001b); for the OMEP Conference (Roche 2003). I carried on with my PhD (Roche 2007) and began to recognise for myself the life-affirming significance of my work for a good democratic society. I presented a paper at the Reading Association of Ireland Conference (Roche 2010) and had a paper included in An Leanbh Óg (OMEP) (Roche 2011b) and hosted several Teacher CPD workshops. I sent a proposal to Routledge which was accepted. My book *Developing Children's Critical Thinking through Picturebooks* was published in 2015 and went on to win an award at UKLA – the United Kingdom Literacy Association.
>
> The book was favourably reviewed in several Literacy journals. This possibly led to my dialogic teaching approach becoming a core module or part of a module on several children's literature and literacy programmes internationally. It is also now a core resource for the Revised Language Curriculum in Ireland (see *Critical Thinking and Book Talk* at www.curriculum online.ie.).

Mary reflects on the process of moving from teacher researcher to becoming an author when she says,

> *It pleases me immensely that my small bit of classroom research has now become available to all Irish primary teachers.*
>
> *I often feel a bit taken aback by how quickly it all happened. But the point of this story is to show that what you think is "ordinary" might be extraordinary to someone else. I often found when reading research papers, that when research was done in classrooms by "ordinary" teachers, somehow, it felt more "real." Perhaps the main reason teachers and teacher educators embraced my work was because it was grounded in real practice. It made sense to them.*

Section 3: Why should I write up and disseminate my educational action research?

Here, we will explore in greater detail the reasons why writing a research report is important and why sharing our research story is an inherent aspect of educational action research.

These issues will be discussed in terms of the role of writing in the research process, the appropriateness of the research account, why we have a responsibility as researchers to share our research story and the importance of amplifying the research voice of the teacher.

The role of writing in the research process

From the opening chapters of this book, you have been encouraged to begin writing. Throughout, you have been urged to refine your thinking as you hone your writing skills. This is because there is an inherent connection between your critical reflection on your practice, your conversations with critical friends and validation groups, and your writing, in the educational action research process. None of these activities take place in isolation – they interlink and develop in connection with each other, and together they ignite your ability to discern your new learning in the research process.

The first notes you make in a reflective journal often capture those ideas that are immediately to the forefront of your thinking at that moment, and often reflect recent dramatic or irritating occurrences in your life. These ideas will always appear in your reflective journal but as you begin to interrogate your own preconceived ideas and engage in meta reflection (as outlined in Chapter 4), you will begin to refine your thinking. Your writing will reflect that too.

So, as you engage in practice writing, which involves drafting and redrafting, you may find that you begin to organise your thoughts somewhat before committing them to paper (or on your screen). Often, teacher-researchers find that those moments of contemplation before writing can help to clarify thinking or to unearth new perspectives and generate new questions. In Section 2, you read how we four authors went about the writing process. We saw first-hand how over time, writing became for us, an instrument through which we questioned our own beliefs and values. Sharing this questioning process with critical friends and discussing it helps us to shape and reshape our ideas and our thinking with more clarity as we bring our reformed ideas back to the writing process again. Here we can see that important link between critical reflection, dialogue and writing taking place.

Because writing, at every stage of the educational action research process, causes us to question and interrogate our innermost thoughts as well as the norms and rules that inform our lives, writing is embedded in the research process (McNiff 2016, McAteer 2013). Therefore, writing can be regarded as a "method of inquiry" and "should be employed as painstakingly as other methods in our research" (Kitchen 2020, p. 236). Take writing seriously and use it to challenge your own fixed views, to hone and craft the ideas as you work towards writing a research account.

We have added a list of sites that can help with academic writing at the end of this chapter.

Appropriateness of your research report

The story of your research can be published in many ways, but it is important that it *is* shared. It can be in the form of a formal written report or article for a journal; an oral presentation; a web-based contribution such as a webinar, blog or a podcast, a poster presentation, or in other forms of presentation.

When you share your research story with others, try to be aware of who the audience is and what information they need to hear. The tone and language of your report or presentation will depend on your audience or readership. If it is a casual, non-formal setting, then your language should reflect this. If it is a more formal setting, then your language should be more formal and academic. Similarly, the content of your report should also reflect the readership or audience. Try to adjust your presentation to suit the needs and the circumstances and also bear in mind that your research is important because it draws on your voice, and it represents the theory that you have generated from your practice.

Some teacher researchers add video and voice recordings of research episodes (with appropriate ethical permissions) to their presentations (see *EJOLTs* for example). This gives the audience a sense of authenticity around the new ideas generated. Others might find that stories from classroom research and artefacts equally contribute to making their research presentations more audience friendly. In poster presentations where internet links are possible, Jack Whitehead has long used the idea of living posters to give a snapshot where one can follow the links to additional sites of practice and research practice (see https://www.actionresearch.net/writings/posters/homepage2021.pdf).

Educational action research reports need not always be in a traditional written format. They can also be represented through the arts. Feldman *et al.* (2018) cite examples from the *Educational Action Research* journal that have been represented through art installations; performance; film and photography and graphic forms of representation. The authors of this book have seen action research reports represented through dance, poetry, story and even cookery. Fisher and Phelps (2006) present their research in the form of a play.

The appropriate tone for academic writing lies in your ability to construct and convey a strong and logical argument. A convincing argument always displays the writer's ability to understand the other side of an argument and to appraise opposing points of view. Although it is important to present your arguments in logical order, your own learning may not be as ordered. In academic writing, writers always interact with each other's texts and so there will be frequent references to the ideas and to the thinking or research of other authors writing in this field. In educational action research this can sometimes mean that literature could be woven throughout the report rather than in a literature review chapter only. This was the case for us authors (see http://www.eari.ie/research-and-publications/).

Regardless of the format of your research report, it is important to remember to report ethically (see Chapter 4). Kalmbach Phillips and Carr (2014, p. 188) remind us that it is not appropriate to share "personal stories that may be harmful to other people by exposing issues, moments, or questions they have not given you permission to share"; accounts of negative incidents written in anger; judgments based solely upon personal opinions and not on evidence. We reiterate that BERA (2018) offers an excellent set of freely accessible ethical guidelines if you are unsure about the ethical aspects of your research report.

Why share your research account?

As teachers, we share our research for many reasons. At a practical level, we share the story of our action research with teacher colleagues because teachers generally like to hear stories of other teachers' new learning. They appreciate the descriptions of new learning as well as the explanations around what happened and the purpose it might serve. Sharing your research is also important to help dispel any unhelpful myths that "teachers can only be consumers of knowledge rather than producers of knowledge of practice" (Feldman *et al.* 2018, p. 256).

Currently, there is a plethora of research being undertaken in classrooms around the world. Much of it is educational action research as it is values-led, values-driven, focused on "I" questions; seeks to enhance practice and aims towards a fairer and more just way of being in the world. It encompasses thousands of hours of critical reflection, engagement with literature, dialogue with critical friends and multitudinous drafts of each account. In other words, it is rigorous, validated research. Yet, as we said at the start of this chapter, few of these accounts are heard in academic circles or within policy-making circles. However, in writing this book on educational action research in the classroom, we are aiming to show how teachers' authentic voices may be heard in conversations and policy-making decisions. There is a list at the end of this chapter of suggested journals and conferences where you might begin to raise your voice and tell others about your research.

McNiff and Whitehead (2006) remind us that teachers' work is largely recognised in terms of practice but not in terms of theory, which brings us back to our remarks in Chapter 1 about the hierarchical and contested nature of knowledge generation. Traditionally teachers were not shown how to conduct research, but this is no longer the case in most jurisdictions. For example, Brennan (2019) brings student teachers' accounts of their pre-service research into the public domain. McNiff and Whitehead (2005) further contend that action research is valuable because it is done by people who ask questions about what they are doing in their everyday work and how they can improve it as a "practical, systematic form of enquiry" (p. 3). They argue (2005, p. 4) that "teachers are powerful creators of theory and should be recognised as such." We agree and we believe that the first real step towards gaining that recognition lies in the dissemination of classroom-based theory and practitioner research accounts. Sharing the research story is vital.

In all fields of research, there is an expectation that results will be shared and made public. The same idea applies to classroom research. Sharing your research with others is a crucial element of the action research process. Whitehead explains that a distinguishing feature of Living Theory research is that the researcher "creates and publicly shares an explanation of their educational influence" (Whitehead 2018, p. 85).

The bulk of research on education is undertaken from an externalist stance and is often large in scale. Many influential research reports are international, funded and inform education policy globally. While this research is very important for helping everyone to understand education better, it is easy for classroom researchers to feel intimidated by the scale and stance of such research. It is important to remember that the more diverse and eclectic the forms of research that are employed in research in education, the clearer and more accurate our understanding of education will be. Therefore, education needs to be informed by reports undertaken from an external stance, but also needs to be informed by the research accounts of the teacher in the classroom who researches their own practice and understands the reality of their own practice more than anyone else. Both forms of research are important and need to co-exist to give a more holistic view of what education entails.

In Chapters 1 and 6, we referred to Schön's (1995) thinking on how practitioner research conflicts with the prevailing epistemology of the research university. Educational action research recognises that teachers are researchers and theorists. Because we generate theory from our practice, and because we are both practitioners *and* researchers/theorists, we can influence the "established canon" and have an influence on the "politics of the control of knowledge" (McNiff 2014, p. 2). Our knowledge is of huge significance. It is important for us as teachers to have our voices heard to inspire new ways of thinking for our profession.

Furthermore, there is a distinct fear that the voice and the knowledge of indigenous cultures are being diminished by the unquestioning acceptance of traditional forms of research. Santos (2014) uses the term "epistemicide" to convey the toxic nature of such research. Thomson (2020, np) explains that academic disciplines in "the global North do not draw on knowledge from the global South. They pay no heed to indigenous knowledges." She further adds that current research conventions "maintain highly restrictive conventions," in terms of knowledge production which are "classed, raced, gendered, heteronormative, neurotypical." As educational action researchers, we have the capacity to challenge these obstacles by telling others about our research account and making sure it is being heard.

Conclusion

In this chapter you encountered many of the ideas and principles of writing up and disseminating educational action research accounts. While research accounts are generally recorded in the form of a written report, there are many other creative formats to present educational action research reports and you can find one appropriate for your setting. The role of writing, in terms of drafting and redrafting, as an integral part of the research process and as a research tool, cannot be underestimated. The dissemination of the story of your learning from the research process is of the utmost importance, not only for having your voice heard by other teachers but to further amplify the classroom teacher's voice within the domain of those who influence policy.

Additional reading suggestions

Kitchen, J. (2020). 'Envisioning writing as a way of knowing in self-study' in Edge, C., Cameron-Standerford, A. and Bergh, B. eds., *Textiles and Tapestries*. EdTech Books, available: https://edtechbooks.org/textiles_tapestries_self_study/chapter_106, 229-237 [accessed 11 April 2022] (Open Access).

Thomson, P. (2020) 'Reading against the literatures', patter, 15 June, available: https://patthomson.net/2020/06/15/reading-against-the-literatures-litreview/ [accessed 12 April 2022] (Blog).

Suggested sites that may help with academic writing

In Ireland resources and supports for academics are provided by the National Universities such as Dublin, Cork, Galway and Maynooth; by many Technical Universities; and by Trinity College Dublin (Fitzmaurice, M. and O'Farrell, C. 2013) and Queen's University Belfast among others.

The library at the University of Leeds, available: https://library.leeds.ac.uk/info/14011/writing/106/academic_writing).

Bob Dick's advice on writing up an action research thesis, available: http://www.aral.com.au/resources/arthesis.html#a_art_writing

Suggested journals for disseminating research

Educational Journal of Living Theories (EJOLTs), available: https://www.ejolts.net/

Educational Action Research Journal, available: https://www.carn.org.uk/journal/

Action Learning and Action Research Journal, available: https://alarj.alarassociation.org

Action Research, available: https://journals.sagepub.com/home/arj

CARN Praxis, available: https://carnpraxis.org/

Professional Development in Education, available: https://ipda.org.uk/professional-development-in-education/

Practice: Contemporary Issues in Practitioner Education available: https://ipda.org.uk/practice-contemporary-issues-in-practitioner-education/

Conclusion

Where to from here?

As a result of reading this book and working your way through the various tasks and exercises, we hope that you have gained an insight into educational action research for the classroom and what values-based research involves. We also hope that you may have begun to think about your practice in a different way. For example, you may now see as challenges things that previously you would have regarded as insurmountable obstacles. You may even feel that it is within your power to enact change in your practice. The ongoing tasks of journaling, reflecting, talking to others and reading have been a constant throughout the book. Continuing these activities can also support you in personalising your own professional development. Taking responsibility for your own professional development may also seem a possibility that you could consider. You might visualise yourself as achieving progress and, in the process, exerting a transformative influence in your practice.

As you develop an action researcherly disposition, as described in Sullivan *et al.* (2016), we hope that engaging in action research may become a way of life for you. Your journey of self-reflection, critical thinking and self-knowledge has greater significance when it is shared with others who may wish to enhance their own practice through undertaking research in it. Having taken the first step in researching your practice through carrying out the suggested tasks in this book, you could have an educational influence in the professional lives of colleagues or friends who may also begin to look at their practice with a more critical lens.

You might consider setting up a group of colleagues, with the aim of continuing to enhance your practice in a collaborative way. You could support one another, either in online or face-to-face meetings, and assist one another in putting research plans into action. You would have easy access to a critical friend, or two, who would provide feedback on your ideas and actions. You would also have a ready-made validation group to assess the quality, rigour and validity of your research efforts. Your cooperative and collaborative undertakings with your colleagues, grounded in a common aim of enhancing practice, could become a community of practice, as described by Wenger (1998). There are several real-life examples of this process in Glenn *et al.* (2017). Perhaps you might like to join a larger network such as our network – the Network for Educational Action Research in Ireland (NEARI).

DOI: 10.4324/9781003288183-9

We hope that you will continue to read professionally and that you will continue to access academic literature. Throughout the book, we have encouraged you to read widely so that your research will be grounded firmly in the theories in the literature. You can be selective around the recommended books, journal articles and online resources in each chapter, and choose to read what appeals to you most. Your thinking and your critical abilities will be greatly enhanced through your engagement with the ideas that you encounter in the literature.

Our learning about key issues for student and teacher education

From working as educational action researchers for almost three decades, we authors have learned that this research approach is of huge benefit to teachers at all stages of the continuum: student teachers, newly qualified teachers, established teachers as well as ourselves. We embraced the approach as mature teachers and found it to be transformational, re-energising and inspirational.

We have worked with teachers across all levels for the past decade and have seen how easily they embraced the educational action research approach: how it made sense to them, how they grew in confidence about their practice and how they developed a strong sense of professionalism and agency. Their research was not just of benefit to them but also to their schools and institutions.

In addition to such transformational possibilities, educational action research can be (i) *viable*, (ii) *optimal*, (iii) *worthwhile*, and (iv) *sustainable* form of research for teachers and student teachers to undertake. Its *viability* lies in that the teacher researcher can investigate real-life situations. You need only focus on what is of importance to your practice. We have found that it is *optimal* in that it is most likely to bring success, new insights or advantage. You have already seen examples of this in some of the teacher researchers' stories in this book. Educational action research is *worthwhile* because it enables you to figure out why things work, or don't, in a rigorous way. That rigour is peer evaluated and subject to critique throughout the process. It also continuously challenges your ideas and seeks to find how they relate to previously existing theories and philosophies. Developing the skill to challenge thinking and actions in classroom research is the key to the *sustainability* of educational action research. The range of teacher researchers' stories in this book has demonstrated the sustainability for beginning researchers up to doctoral level. There are also many accounts of teachers whose research did not progress in the manner they wanted, but who were able to revise their thinking and generate new learning about themselves, their institution and the education system.

Teacher voice

The voice of the teacher-researcher in the classroom is not being widely heard in academic or policy-making circles. Yet their research has had an invaluable influence at a personal and local level, in classrooms, and school settings. It is seriously concerning to see how few teachers choose to present their research in public or academic settings.

Likewise, very few publish in professional academic journals. The most common platform seems to be in "tips or tricks" contexts. Perhaps now, you can consider how you might begin to make a difference here.

We believe that now is the time for teachers to collectively have their voices heard, to share the reality of their workplaces using their own research from their classrooms and to demand that their professionalism be treated with the respect that it deserves. We invite *you* to take that first step in that process.

A note to teacher educators

If you are a teacher educator, we hope that having read this book, you may be encouraged now to use an educational action research approach with your students. We authors are fully convinced of the power that undertaking educational action research can have for developing agency and self-confidence in students' chosen professions. We also hope you may be motivated to begin investigating and enhancing your own practice as a teacher educator, which would further help you to help your students.

Assessing educational action research may present challenges for accrediting institutions. We suggest that a multi-modal approach to assessment has proved the most successful. In addition to a written report, discursive vivas with external and staff members, as well as presentations at various stages of the process can often bring the passionate learning of teacher researchers to the fore.

A note to all teachers

People still generally enter teaching with a wish to make a difference. Unfortunately, that motivation can be eroded when people lose their sense of professional identity and autonomy, as is the case when the current culture of "increased accountability and appraisal, and feeling that 'nothing is good enough' reflects a recurrent theme of self-doubt" (Sturrock 2021, p. 31). While we understand that undertaking educational action research is not a magic potion to cure all ills, it has been shown again and again that it strengthens teachers' sense of professional identity and autonomy.

The threat to teacher professionalism is strong – and we accept the contested nature of professionalism. Mayer and Mills (2021) argue that "policy imperatives fail to acknowledge the importance of enhancing the research literacy of teachers or to prepare new teachers to become teacher-researchers" (p. 45). We believe that this book will encourage you to see beyond these challenges.

Final words

We hope that by examining their practice, teachers can design and personalise their own CPD as they create their personal living educational theory. By improving or enhancing what they do, by understanding better what they do, by being able to provide a rationale for why they do what they do, they can improve the quality of their lives for their own learning and create better learning opportunities for themselves and for those with whom they work.

The array of teacher researchers' stories in this book demonstrates the sustainability of educational action research for the continuum of teachers who conduct research in their classrooms – from beginner researchers to doctoral level. We authors are convinced that researching your own practice in order to enhance or improve what you do for the benefit of others is pivotal to the creation of a better and more just society – and we invite you now to begin the process of doing just that!

Bibliography

Agud, I. and Ion, G. (2019) 'Research-based learning in initial teacher education in Catalonia', *CEPS Journal*, 9(2), 99-118, available: 10.26529/cepsj.564

Al Riyami, T. (2015) 'Main approaches to educational research', *International Journal of Innovation and Research in Educational Science*, 2(5), 2349-5219, available: https://www.ijires.org/administrator/components/com_jresearch/files/publications/IJIRES_361_Final.pdf, [accessed 6 August 2022].

Ball, S.J. (2003) 'The teacher's soul and the terrors of performativity', *Journal of Education Policy*, 18(2), 215-228, available: 10.1080/0268093022000043065

Baskerville, D. and Goldblatt, H. (2009) 'Learning to be a critical friend: from professional indifference through challenge to unguarded conversations', *Cambridge Journal of Education*, 39(2), 205-221, available: 10.1080/0268093022000043065

Bassey, M. (1990) *On the Nature of Research in Education*, Nottingham: Nottingham Polytechnic.

Bassey, M. (1999) *Case Study Research in Educational Settings*, Birmingham: Open University Press.

BERA (British Educational Research Association) (2018) *Ethical Guidelines for Educational Research*, 4th ed., available: https://www.bera.ac.uk/publication/ethical-guidelines-for-educational-research-2018-online [accessed 1 May 2022].

Bourdieu, P. (1990) *The Logic of Practice*, Cambridge: Polity.

Bohm, D. (2004) *On Dialogue*, Oxon: Routledge Classics.

Bradbury, H., Waddell, S., O'Brien, K., Apgar, M., Teehankee, B. and Fazey, I. (2019) 'A call to action research for transformations: The times demand it', *Action Research*, 17(1), 3-10, available: 10.1177/1476750319829633

Bradbury-Jones, C. and Taylor, J. (2015) 'Engaging with children as co-researchers: challenges, counter-challenges and solutions', *International Journal of Social Research Methodology*, 18(2), 161-173, available: 10.1080/13645579.2013.864589

Braun, V. and Clarke, V. (2006) 'Using thematic analysis in psychology', *Qualitative Research in Psychology*, 3(2), 77-101, available: 10.1191/1478088706qp063oa

Brennan, A. (2019) 'Student Teacher Educational Research (STER): An innovation in Irish Teacher Education', *Education Research and Perspectives, An International Journal University of Western Australia* (46), 44-74. available: 10.3316/ielapa.060631707100635

Brookfield, S.D. (2017) *Becoming a Critically Reflective Teacher*, 2nd ed., San Francisco, U.S.A.: Wiley/Jossey-Bass.

Bruce Ferguson, P. (2015) 'Who am I who teaches?', *Educational Journal of Living Theories*, 8(1), 49-66, available: https://www.ejolts.net/files/Bruce_Ferguson8%281%29.pdf., [accessed 21 July 2022].

Brydon-Miller, M., Greenwood, D. and Maguire, P. (2003) 'Why action research?', *Action Research*, 1(1), 9-28.

Burbules, N.C. (2000) 'At the limits of dialogue as critical pedagogy' in Trifonas, P.P., ed., *Revolutionary Pedagogies: Cultural Politics, Instituting Education, and the Discourse of Theory*, New York: RoutledgeFalmer, 251-274.

Carr, W. and Kemmis, S. (1986) *Becoming Critical: Education, Knowledge and Action Research*, London: Falmer Press.

Carozzi, G. (2019) 'A self-enquiry: towards the development of my living-educational-theory research', *Educational Journal of Living Theories*, 12(2), 36-64, available: https://ejolts.net/files/348.pdf, [accessed 25 July 2022].

Chatterjee, R. (2022) *Happy Mind, Happy Life: 10 Simple Ways to Feel Great Every Day*, London: Penguin Books.

Chiennat, S. (2015) 'Internship in pre-service teacher education programme: A global perspective', *International Journal of Research in Applied, Natural and Social Sciences* (IMPACT), 2(11), 79-94.

Clark, C. (2001) *Talking Shop: Authentic Conversation and Teacher Learning*, New York: Teachers College Press.

Clark, J.S., Porath, S., Thiele, J. and Jobe, M. (2020) *Action Research*, NPP eBooks 34, available: https://newprairiepress.org/ebooks/34, [accessed 6 August 2022].

Clarke, A. and Erikson, G. (2006) 'Teacher inquiry: What's old is new again!', *BC Educational Leadership Research*, 6, 1-8, available: https://blogs.ubc.ca/stevemcg/files/2015/09/Clarke-Erickson-2006.-Teacher-inquiry-Whats-old-is-new-again.pdf, [accessed 5 August 2022].

Coghlan, D. (2022) 'Building and Enhancing Quality in Organizational Action Research', Paper presented at *10th International Action Research Colloquium of the Action Research Group Ireland (ARGI))* at TU Dublin, 23 -24 June.

Coghlan, D. and Brannick, T. (2005) *Doing Action Research in Your Own Organization*, 2nd ed., London: Sage Publications.

Cohen, L., Manion, L. and Morrison, K. (2018) *Research Methods in Education*, 8th ed., London: Taylor Francis/Routledge.

Connaughton, A. (2021) *How Can I, as a Froebelian Teacher, Practise Active and Experiential Learning in an Irish Language Early Immersion Education (Luath-Tumoideachas) Setting?* unpublished thesis (M.Ed.), National University of Ireland Maynooth.

Cook, T. (2009) 'The purpose of mess in action research: Building rigour through a messy turn', *Educational Action Research*, 17(2), 277-291, available: 10.1080/09650790902914241

Costa, A.L. and Kallik, B. (1993) 'Through the lens of a critical friend', *Educational Leadership*, 51(2), 49-51.

Creswell, J.W. (2007) *Qualitative Inquiry and Research Design: Choosing among Five Approaches*, 2nd ed., Thousand Oaks, CA: Sage Publications.

CROI n.d. 'Research Strategy' in Teaching Council of Ireland, ed., *Collaboration and Research for Ongoing Innovation*, available: https://www.teachingcouncil.ie/en/_fileupload/research/research-strategy-updated.pdf, [accessed 20 July 2022].

Dadds, M. and Hart, S. (2001) *Doing Practitioner Research Differently*, London: RoutledgeFalmer.

Davison, N. (2015) 'Friday Five: Things teachers miss out on because they're too busy', Times Educational Supplement, 4 December, available: https://www.tes.com/magazine/archive/friday-five-things-teachers-miss-out-because-theyre-too-busy [accessed 6 August 2022].

Department of Children and Youth Affairs (2017) *Guidance for Developing Ethical Research Projects Involving Children*, Dublin: Irish Government.

Deasy, C. and Mannix McNamara, P. (2016) 'Challenging performativity in higher education: Promoting a healthier learning culture' in Renes, S., ed., *Global Voices in Higher Education*, available: https://www.intechopen.com/chapters/55240 [accessed 5 August 2022].

Delong, J. (2020) 'Raising voices using dialogue as a research method for creating living-educational-theories in cultures of inquiry', *Educational Journal of Living Theories*, 13(2), 71-92, available: https://ejolts.net/files/4Jackie367.pdf, [accessed 6 August 2022].

Demetriou, H. (2018) *Empathy, Emotion & Education*, Cambridge: Palgrave Macmillan.

Dewey, J. (1933) *How We Think: A Restatement of the Relation of Reflective Thinking in the Educative Process*, Boston, MA: D.C. Heath.

Dick, B. (n.d.) *Action Research and Evaluation on Line (AREOL)*, available: http://www.aral.com.au/areol/areolind.html, [accessed 11 September 2022].

Dickens, C. (1854) *Hard Times*, From Dickens Household Words, Weeks 1 to 20. New York: T. L. McElrath and Co Publishers.

Education Week (2022) 'This Year's Most Influential Education Scholars (in Charts)', *Education Week*, 18 January, available: https://www.edweek.org/policy-politics/opinion-this-years-most-influential-education-scholars-in-charts/2022/01 [accessed 6 August 2022].

EU Academy (n.d.) *Teachers as Researchers - Improving Classroom Practice through Action Research*, available: https://academy.europa.eu/courses/teachers-as-researchers-improving-classroom-practice-through-action-research-1658151350, [accessed 19 September 2022].

Famakinwa, J.O. (2012), 'Is the unexamined life worth living or not?', *Think, Philosophy for Everyone*, 11(31), 97-103, available: 10.1017/S1477175612000073

Feldman, A., Altrichter, H., Posch, P. and Somekh, B. (2018) *Teachers Investigate their Work: An Introduction to Action Research across the Professions*, 3rd ed., London: Routledge.

Fisher, K. and Phelps, R. (2006) 'Recipe or performing art? Challenging conventions for writing action research theses', *Action Research*, 4(2), 143-164, available: 10.1177/1476750306063989

Fitz, J.A. and Nikolaidis, A.C. (2020) 'A democratic critique of scripted curriculum', *Journal of Curriculum Studies*, 52(2), 195-213, available: 10.1080/00220272.2019.1661524

Frankl, V.E. (1972) 'Existential Escapism', *OMEGA - Journal of Death and Dying*, 2(4), 307-311, available: 10.2190/JKVQ-YTQV-VLDV-3JKL

Frankl, V.E. (2004) *Man's Search For Meaning*, London: Rider.

Freire, P. (1972) *Pedagogy of the Oppressed*, London: Sheed and Ward.

Freire, P. (1985) 'Reading the world and reading the word: An interview with Paulo Freire', *Language Arts*, 62, 15-21, available: https://www.jstor.org/stable/i40068332 [accessed 5 August 2022].

Freire, P. (1990) *Pedagogy of the Oppressed*. New York: Continuum

Freire, P. (2005) *Pedagogy of the Oppressed, 30th Anniversary Edition*, New York: Continuum.

Fromm, E. (1960) *Fear of Freedom*, London: Routledge and Kegan Paul.

Gamage, K.A.A., Dehideniya, D.M.S.C.P.K. and Ekanayake, S.Y. (2021) 'The role of personal values in learning approaches and student achievements', *Behavioural Sciences*, 11(7), 102, available: 10.3390/bs11070102

Giroux, H. (2011) *On Critical Pedagogy*, New York: Continuum.

Glenn, M. (2006) *Working with Collaborative Projects: My Living Theory of a Holistic Educational Practice*, unpublished thesis (Ph.D.), University of Limerick.

Glenn, M. (2016) 'Warning: Action Research may be for life – not just a project', presented at *Collaborative Action Research Network International Conference*, Bishop Grosseteste University, Lincoln, 11-13 November.

Glenn, M. (2021a) Extending knowledge by developing a 'slow approach' to action research, *Educational Action Research*, 10.1080/09650792.2021.1948434

Glenn, M. (2021b) 'What is the educational influence of my engagement with EJOLTs (Educational Journal of Living Theories)?', *Educational Journal of Living Theories*, 14(1), 50-67, available: https://www.ejolts.net/files/373.pdf, [accessed 6 August 2022].

Glenn, M., McDonagh, C., Sullivan, B. and Roche, M. with M. Morgan (2012) '*Practice-based Research Encompassing Professional Development Project: Final report March 2012*', available: https://www.teachingcouncil.ie/en/Publications/Research/Documents/Practice-based-Research-Encompassing-Professional-Development-Project.pdf., [accessed 6 June 2022].

Glenn, M., Roche, M., McDonagh, C. and Sullivan, B. (2017) *Learning Communities in Educational Partnerships*, London and New York: Bloomsbury.

Glenn, M., Connolly, C., McDonagh, C., Sullivan, B. and Roche, M. (2022) 'Enkindling Educational Influence', presented at *10th International Action Research Colloquium of the Action Research Group Ireland (ARGI)* at TU Dublin June 23-24th.

Gonzalez, J., Farrell, J. and Auguste, S. (2021) 'A portrait of becoming: Transformative teacher education through an offshore location in the Bahamas', *Educational Journal of Living Theories*, 14(2), 1-25, available: https://ejolts.net/files/378.pdf, [accessed 25 July 2022].

Goodwin, A.L. (2021) 'Teaching standards, globalisation, and conceptions of teacher professionalism', *European Journal of Teacher Education*, 44 (1), 5-19, available: 10.1080/02619768.2020.1833855

Gorman, A. (2021) *The Hill We Climb: Poems*. Penguin Random House Group.

Government of Ireland (1998) *Education Act*, Dublin: Stationery Office.

Government of Ireland (2000) *Education Welfare Act*, Dublin: Stationery Office.

Gramsci, A. (1971) *Selections from the Prison Notebooks of Antonio Gramsci*, New York: International Publishers.

Greene, M. (1980) 'Aesthetics and the experience of the arts: Towards transformations', *The High School Journal*, 63(8), 316-322, available: http://www.jstor.org/stable/40365004. [accessed 5 August 2022].

Greene, M. (1984) 'How we think about the craft of teaching', *Teachers College Record*, 86(1), 55-67, available: https://maxinegreene.org/uploads/, [accessed 5 August 2022].

Greene, M. (1995) *Releasing the Imagination: Essays on Education, The Arts and Social Change*, San Francisco: Jossey-Bass.

Griffin, C. and Delong, J. (2021) 'As educators and educational researchers, what contribution has a living educational theory approach made to helping us to improve the quality of our practice and our lives?', *Educational Journal of Living Theories*, 14(1), 26–49, available: https://ejolts.net/files/372.pdf, [accessed 25 July 2022].

Gumede, J.T. (2020) 'Living educational theory development of a Black African (Zulu) male educator', *Educational Journal of Living Theories*, 13(1), 1-21, available: https://ejolts.net/files/354.pdf, [accessed 25 July 2022].

Habermas, J. (1976) *Communication and the Evolution of Society* (trans. McCarthy, 1979), London: Beacon Press.

Hamilton, M.L. and Pinnegar, S. (2014) 'Self-Study of Teacher Education Practices as a Pedagogy for Teacher Educator Professional Development', *International Teacher Education: Promising Pedagogies (Part A) (Advances in Research on Teaching)*, 137–152, available: 10.1108/S1479-368720140000022010

Hartog, M. (2004) *A self-study of a higher education tutor: how can I improve my practice?* unpublished thesis (PhD), University of Bath, available: https://www.actionresearch.net/living/hartog.shtml, [accessed 5 August 2022].

Heaney, S. (1984) *Station Island*, London: Faber and Faber.

Herr, K.G. and Anderson, G. (2015) *The Action Research Dissertation: A Guide for Students and Faculty*, 2nd ed., Thousand Oaks: Sage Publications.

Hickey, C. (2018) 'History of Action Research in Education', *The Centre for Effective Services (CES)*, available: https://www.teachingcouncil.ie/en/research-croi-/research-webinars-/past-webinars/ethics-webinar-slides.pdf, [accessed 6 August 2022].

Hiebert, J., Gallimore, R. and Stigler, J.W. (2002) 'A knowledge base for the teaching profession: What would it look like and how can we get one?', *Educational Researcher*, 31(5), 3-15, 10.3102/0013189X031005003

Hilsen, A.I. (2006) 'And they shall be known by their deeds: Ethics and politics in action research', *Action Research*, 4(1), 23-36, 10.1177/1476750306060539

Hodgins, M., and Mannix-McNamara, P. (2021) 'The Neoliberal University in Ireland: Institutional bullying by another name?', *Societies (Basel, Switzerland)*, 11(2), 52, available: 10.3390/soc11020052

Hogan, P. (2011) 'The ethical orientations of education as a practice in its own right', *Ethics and Education*, 6(1), 26-40, available: 10.1080/17449642.2011.587345

Hoyle, E. (1975) 'Professionality, professionalism and control in teaching' in Houghton, V., McHugh, R. and Morgan C., eds., *Management in Education: The Management of Organisations and Individuals*, London: Ward Lock Educational in association with Open University Press.

Hughes, I. and William, R. (2001) *Planning Your Action Research Project*, available: https://studylib.net/doc/7489002/what-is-action-research--ar-%3F [accessed 13 July 2022].

İnözü, J. (2017) 'Drawings are talking: Exploring language learners' beliefs through visual narratives', *Applied Linguistics Review*, 9(2), 177-200, available: 10.1515/applirev-2016-1062

Irvine, S. and Price, J. (2014) 'Professional conversations: A collaborative approach to support policy implementation, professional learning and practice change in ECEC', *Australasian Journal of Early Childhood*, 39(3), 85-93, available: 10.1177/183693911403900311

Johnson, A.P. (2012) *A Short Guide to Action Research*, 4th ed, New York: Pearson Education.

Joynt, G. (2019) *How Can I Nurture Compassion in my Classroom?* unpublished thesis (M.Ed. Research in Practice), Maynooth University, available: https://mural.maynoothuniversity.ie/13705/

Kalmbach Phillips, D. and Carr, K. (2014) *Becoming a Teacher through Action Research: Process, Context, and Self-Study*, 3rd ed., New York: Routledge.

Kelchtermans, G. (2009) 'Who I am in how I teach is the message: self-understanding, vulnerability and reflection', *Teacher and Teaching: Theory and Practice*, 15(2), 257-272, available: 10.1080/13540600902875332

Kemmis, S. (2009) 'Action research as a practice-based practice', *Educational Action Research*, 17(3), 463-474, available: 10.1080/09650790903093284

Kemmis, S. (2012) 'Researching educational praxis: spectator and participant perspectives', *British Educational Research Journal*, 38(6), 885-905, available: 10.1080/01411926.2011.588316

Kemmis, S. (2022) 'Transforming Practices', *NEARIMeet Online*, [video], available: http://www.eari.ie/2022/02/08/notes-from-nearimeet-29-january-2022/ [accessed 6 August 2022].

Kemmis, S. and McTaggart, R. (2000) 'Participatory action research' in Denzin, N.K. and Lincoln, Y.S., eds., *Handbook of Qualitative Research*, 2nd ed., Thousand Oaks, CA: Sage, 567–607.

Kemmis, S., McTaggart, R. and Nixon, R. (2014) *The Action Research Planner: Doing critical participatory action research*, Singapore: Springer.

Kitchen, J. (2020) 'Envisioning writing as a way of knowing in self-study' in Edge, C., Cameron-Standerford, A. and Bergh, B., eds., *Textiles and Tapestries*, EdTech Books, 229–237, available: https://edtechbooks.org/textiles_tapestries_self_study/chapter_106, [accessed 11 April 2022].

Ledwith, M. (2017) 'Emancipatory action research as a critical living praxis: From dominant narratives to counternarratives' in Rowell, L.L., Bruce, C., Shosh, J.M. and Riel, M.M., eds., *The Palgrave International Handbook of Action Research*, 21–35, New York: Palgrave Macmillan.

Leitch, R. (2018) 'On being transgressive in educational research! An autoethnography of borders', *Irish Educational Studies*, 37(2), 159–174, available: 10.1080/03323315.2018.1471412

Lewin, K. (1946) 'Action research and minority problems', *Journal of Social Issues*, 2, 34–46, available: 10.1111/j.1540-4560.1946.tb02295.x

Lingard, B. and Renshaw, P. (2010) 'Teaching as research-informed and research-informing profession' in Campbell, A. and Groundwater-Smith, S., eds., *Connecting Inquiry and Professional Learning in Education*, London: Routledge, 40–53, available: 10.4324/9780203609453-9

Lortie, D.C. (1975) *Schoolteacher: A Sociological Study*, Chicago: University of Chicago Press.

Lummis, G.W., Morris, J.E., Ferguson, C., Hill, S. and Lock, G. (2022) 'Leadership teams supporting teacher wellbeing by improving the culture of an Australian secondary school', *Issues in Educational Research*, 32(1), 205–224.

Mavhunga, E. and Merwe, D.V.D. (2020) 'Bridging science education's theory–practice divide: A perspective from teacher education through topic-specific PCK', *African Journal of Research in Mathematics, Science and Technology Education*, 24(1), 65–80, available: https://doi-org.jproxy.nuim.ie/10.1080/18117295.2020.1716496

Marsh, S. (2015) 'Five top reasons people become teachers – and why they quit', *The Guardian*, 27 Jan, available: https://www.theguardian.com/teacher-network/2015/jan/27/five-top-reasons-teachers-join-and-quit [accessed 5 August 2022].

Massó-Guijarro, B. (2021) 'Dialogue in education: A strong commitment to social and educational transformation', *The International Journal of Pedagogy and Curriculum*, 28(2), 85–93.

Mayer, D. and Mills, M. (2021) 'Professionalism and teacher education in Australia and England', *European Journal of Teacher Education*, 44(1), 45–61, available: 10.1080/02619768.2020.1832987.Rose

McAteer, M. (2013) *Action Research in Education*, London: Sage.

McAteer, M. (2020) 'The Values-based Researcher: a state of (constantly) becoming', *NEARIMeet Online*, [video], available: http://www.eari.ie/2020/10/14/notes-from-nearimeet-19-september-2020-online/, [accessed 1 August 2022].

McDonagh, C. (2017) 'Validity', *Presentation at NEARIMeet*, [video], available: https://youtu.be/tLs_ItgxeUw, [accessed 1 August 2022].

McDonagh, C. and Sullivan, B. (2017) 'Living research: How do we realise our capacity to create knowledge as we live towards our professional values in our practice?', *Educational Journal of Living Theories*, 10(1), 26–42, available: https://ejolts.net/files/2.pdf, [accessed 1 August 2022].

McDonagh, C., Roche, M., Sullivan, B. and Glenn, M. (2012) *Enhancing Practice through Classroom Research: A Teacher's Guide to Professional Development*, Abingdon: Routledge.

McDonagh, C., Roche, M., Sullivan, B. and Glenn, M. (2020) *Enhancing Practice through Classroom Research: A Teacher's Guide to Professional Development*, 2nd ed., Abingdon: Routledge.

McNiff, J. (n.d.) *Action Research for Professional Development*, 3rd ed., available: https://www.jeanmcniff.com/ar-booklet.asp [accessed 12 July 2022].

McNiff, J. (2010) *Action Research for Professional Development: Concise Advice for New (and Experienced) Action Researchers*, Dorset: September Books.

McNiff, J. (2014) *Writing and Doing Action Research*, London: Sage Publications.

McNiff, J. (2016) *Writing up Your Action Research Project*, Abingdon: Routledge.

McNiff, J. and Whitehead, J. (2005) *Action Research for Teachers: A Practical Guide*, London: David Fulton Publishers Ltd.

McNiff, J. and Whitehead, J. (2006) *All You Need to Know about Action Research*, London: Sage.

McNiff, J. and Whitehead, J. (2009) *You and Your Action Research Project*, 3rd ed. London, New York: Routledge.

McNiff, J. and Whitehead, J. (2011) *All You Need to Know about Action Research*, 2nd ed., London: Sage Publications Ltd.

McNiff, J., Edvardsen, O. and Steinholt, M. (2018) '"Impact", educational influence and the practice of shared expertise', *Educational Action Research*, 26(5), 803-819, available: 10.1080/09650792.2018.1426469

Mellor, N. (2001) 'Messy method: The unfolding story', *Educational Action Research*, 9(3): 465-484, available: 10.1080/09650790100200166

Moeller, J., Ivcevic, Z., White, A.E., Menges, J.I. and Brackett, M.A. (2018) 'Highly engaged but burned out: intra-individual profiles in the US workforce', *Career Development International*, 23(1), 86-105, available: 10.1108/CDI-12-2016-0215

Mounter, J. (2008) *How can I work within the government's perspective of 'Gifted and Talented' but still remain true to my own living values?* unpublished master's assignment, University of Bath, available: https://www.actionresearch.net/writings/tuesdayma/jmgt2008opt.pdf, [accessed 2 August 2022].

Mounter, J. (2012) *As a Headteacher Researcher how can I demonstrate the impact and self-understandings drawn from Living Theory Action Research, as a form of Continual Professional Development in education?* unpublished thesis (Masters), University of Bath, available: https://actionresearch.net/writings/module/joymounterma.pdf, [accessed 2 August 2022].

Mounter, J. (2019) 'An original contribution, ~i~we~I~us~ Relationships', available: http://www.spanglefish.com/allicanbe/index.asp?pageid=698540, [accessed 30 July 2022].

Mounter, J. (2021) *Transfer of registration from Probationary to Confirmed PhD or MPhil to PhD (draft)*, available: https://www.actionresearch.net/writings/mounter/joydrafttransfer280221.pdf, [accessed 2 August 2022].

Muñoz-Arce, G. and Rubilar-Donoso, G. (2021) 'Social work research in Chile: Tensions and challenges under the "Knowledge Economy" and Managerialist Research Agendas', *The British Journal of Social Work*, 51(7), 2839-2856, available: 10.1093/bjsw/bcaa132

Noddings, N. (1995) 'Care and moral education' in Kohli, W., ed., *Critical Conversations in Philosophy of Education*, Abington: Routledge.

Oancea, A. (2014) 'Teachers' professional knowledge and state-funded teacher education: a (hi)story of critiques and silences', *Oxford Review of Education*, 40(4), 497-519, available: 10.1080/03054985.2014.939413

O'Donnell, C. (2021) *Developing Children's Vocabulary and Expressive Language Skills Through Play*, unpublished thesis (Masters), National University of Ireland Maynooth. available: https://mural.maynoothuniversity.ie/15168/ [accessed 5 August 2022].

O'Donohue, J. (2003) *Divine Beauty: The Invisible Embrace*, London: Transworld Publishers.

O'Farrell, H. (2018) *How Can I Develop Children's Empathy through the Implementation of a Fictional Literature Programme?* unpublished thesis (Masters), National University of Ireland Maynooth, available: https://mural.maynoothuniversity.ie/13717/ [accessed 5 August 2022].

Palmer, P. (n.d.) *The Heart of a Teacher: Identity and Integrity in Teaching*, available: https://couragerenewal.org/library/the-heart-of-a-teacher/ [accessed 2 September 2022] (Open Access)

Palmer, P.J. (2017) *The Courage to Teach: Exploring the Inner Landscape of a Teacher's Life* (20th Anniversary Ed), San Francisco: Jossey Bass.

Pepper, J. (2022) @gillian_pepper *Reading the news coverage of the @UCU #FourFights strike, I get the impression that many people don't know what University lecturers do (and why would they?), so here's a thread on it.*[Twitter] 28 February 15.42, available: https://twitter.com/gillian_pepper/status/1498322672291393545 [accessed 5 August 2022].

Peters, R.S. (1966) *Ethics and Education*, London: Allen & Unwin.

Petrarca, D. and Van Nuland, S. (2020) 'Initial Teacher Education Practicum 2.0' in Kitchen, J., Berry, A., Bullock, S.M., Crowe, A.R., Taylor, M., Guðjónsdóttir, H. and Thomas, L. eds., *International Handbook of Self-study of Teaching and Teacher Education Practices*, Singapore: Springer, 1103-1130.

Pithouse, K., Mitchell, C. and Weber, S. (2009) 'Self-study in teaching and teacher development: a call to action', *Educational Action Research*, 17(1), 43-62, available: 10.1080/09650790802667444

Polanyi, M. (1958) *Personal Knowledge: Towards a Post Critical Philosophy*, London: Routledge.

Polanyi, M. (1962) *Personal Knowledge*, New York: Harper Torchbooks.

Polanyi, M. (1966) *The Tacit Knowledge*, Chicago: The University of Chicago Press.

Polanyi, M. (1969) *Knowing and Being: Essays by Michael Polanyi*, Chicago: The University of Chicago Press.

Rahmann, M.H., Lund, T., Alamin, M., Khalid Mujib, A. and Krogh, E. (2021) 'Developing a transformative, cooperative living-educational-theory with children and youth in the EDS (Education for Development and Sustainability) community of practice in Bangladesh', *Educational Journal of Living Theories*, 14(2), 26-50, available: https://www.ejolts.net/files/379.pdf, [accessed 2 August 2022].

Rauch, F., Zehetmeier, S. and Posch, P. (2019) 'Educational action research' in Zuber-Skerritt, O. and Wood, L., eds., *Action Learning and Action Research: Genres and Approaches*, 111-126, available: 10.1108/978-1-78769-537-520191012

Ravitch, D. (2022) 'Kathryn Joyce: Arizona Eliminates Standards for Teachers', *Diane Ravitch's Blog*, 13 July, available: https://dianeravitch.net/2022/07/13/kathryn-joyce-arizona-eliminates-standards-for-teachers/ [accessed 13 July 2022].

Rawls, (1971) *A Theory of Justice*, London: Oxford University Press.

Riel, M. (n.d.) *Action Research Tutorials*, available: https://www.actionresearchtutorials.org/, [accessed 11 September 2022]

Robertson, J. (2000) 'The three Rs of action research methodology: reciprocity, reflexivity and reflection-on-reality', *Educational Action Research*, 8(2), 307-326, available: 10.1080/09650790000200124

Roche, M. (2001a) 'Fishes think about lorries', *InTouch*, 30(4), 23-25.

Roche, M. (2001b) 'Fishes think about lorries: a primary teacher's experience of classroom discussion' *'arista' Journal of the Association of Teachers for Philosophy with Children*, 1(2), 82-89.

Roche, M. (2003) 'Setting the "what if" free', in *Transformations – Theory and Practice: Conference Proceedings OMEP*, University College Cork.

Roche, M. (2007) *Towards a Living Theory of Caring Pedagogy: interrogating my practice to nurture a critical, emancipatory, and just community of enquiry*, unpublished thesis (PhD), University of Limerick, available: http://www.eari.ie/research-and-publications/mary-roches-phd-thesis/ [accessed 12 July 2022].

Roche, M. (2010) '"Critical Thinking and Book Talk": Using picturebooks to promote discussion and critical thinking in the classroom', *Reading News* (Conference Edition), Dublin.

Roche, M. (2011a) 'Creating a dialogical and critical classroom: Reflection and action to improve practice', *Educational Action Research*, 19(3), 327-343, available: 10.1080/09650792.2011.600607

Roche, M. (2011b) 'A Self-study Action Research Approach towards Developing Dialogic Pedagogies that Support Children's Capacity to Think Critically', *An Leanbh Óg*, The OMEP Ireland Journal of Early Childhood Studies, Vol 4 and Vol 5, June 2011, edited by Rosaleen Murphy, 141-158.

Roche, M. (2015) *Developing Children's Critical Thinking through Picturebooks: A Guide for Primary and Early Years Students and Teachers*, Abingdon: Routledge.

Rogers, C.B. and Freiberg, H.J. (1994) *Freedom to Learn*, 3rd ed., New Jersey: Prentice Hall.

Rose, N. (2015) 'Ethical issues in teacher-led research', *Evidence into Practice: a blog about evidence-informed teaching*, available: https://evidenceintopractice.wordpress.com/2015/04/05/ethical-issues-in-teacher-led-research/ [accessed 1 May 2022].

Rosenblatt, L. (1978) *The Reader, the Text, the Poem: The Transactional Theory of the Literary Work*, Carbondale, IL: Southern Illinois University Press.

Rosenblatt, L.M. (1994) 'The transactional theory of reading and writing' in Ruddell, R.B., Ruddell, M.R. and Singer, H., eds., *Theoretical Models and Processes of Reading*, 1057-1092, International Reading Association.

Rowell, L., and Feldman, A. (2019) 'Knowledge democracy and action research', *Educational Action Research*, available: 10.1080/09650792.2019.1557456

Sachs, J. (2016) 'Teacher professionalism: why are we still talking about it?', *Teachers and Teaching, Theory and Practice*, 22(4), 413-425, available: 10.1080/13540602.2015.1082732

Santos, B.D.S. (2014) *Epistemologies of the South: Justice against Epistemicide*, London: Paradigm Publishers.

Schön, D.A. (1995) 'Knowing-in-action: The new scholarship requires a new epistemology', *Change the Magazine of Higher Learning*, 27(6), 27-34, available: 10.1080/00091383.1995.10544673

Schuk, S. and Russell, T. (2005) 'Studying teacher education: A journal of self-study, critical friendship, and the complexities of teacher education', *Studying Teacher Education*, 1(2), 107-121, available: 10.1080/1742596050288291

Sen, A. (2009) 'Foreward' in Polanyi, M., *The Tacit Dimension*, Chicago: The University of Chicago Press, vii–xvi.

Shulman, L.S. (1999) 'Taking learning seriously', *The Magazine of Higher Learning*, 31(4), 10–17, available: 10.1080/00091389909602695

Smith, M.K. (2003) 'Michael Polanyi and tacit knowledge', *The encyclopedia of pedagogy and informal education*, available: https://infed.org/mobi/michael-polanyi-and-tacit-knowledge/, [accessed 11 September 2022].

Storey, V.A. and Beeman, T.E. (2009) 'Values to action: Utilizing a value informed decision matrix to "jumpstart" dialogue and critical self reflection by school leaders on elements influencing their decision-making process', *Journal of Alternative Perspectives in the Social Sciences*, 1(3), 760–782.

Sturrock, S. (2021): 'Primary teachers' experiences of neo-liberal education reform in England: "Nothing is ever good enough"', *Research Papers in Education* (ahead of print) 1–27, available: 10.1080/02671522.2021.1941213

Sullivan, B., Glenn, M., Roche, M. and McDonagh, C. (2016) *Introduction to Critical Reflection and Action for Teacher Researchers*, Abingdon: Routledge.

Sullivan, B., Roche, M., Glenn, M., and McDonagh, C. (2021) 'Practitioner enquiry and action research for teacher well-being' in Murphy, T.R.N. and Mannix-McNamara, P., eds., *International Perspectives on Teacher Well-being and Diversity*, Singapore: Springer.

Sullivan, B., McDonagh, C., Connolly, C., Glenn, M. and Roche, M. (2022) 'Exploring trans-generational and trans-institutional learning: educational action research possibilities in a virtual environment', *Irish Educational Studies*, available: 10.1080/03323315.2022.2043175

Swaffield, S. (2008) 'Critical friendship, dialogue and learning, in the context of leadership for learning', *School Leadership & Management*, 28(4), 323–336, available: 10.1080/13632430802292191

Teaching Council of Ireland (2016a) *Code of Professional Practice: Updated 2nd Edition*, available: https://www.teachingcouncil.ie/en/publications/fitness-to-teach/code-of-professional-conduct-for-teachers1.pdf., [accessed 7 August 2022].

Teaching Council of Ireland (2016b) *Droichead: An Integrated Induction Framework for Newly Qualified Teachers*, Maynooth: Teaching Council Ireland.

Teaching Council of Ireland (2017) *Initial Teacher Education: Criteria and Guidelines for Programme Providers*, Revised Edition, Maynooth: Teaching Council of Ireland.

Thomson, P. (2020) 'Reading against the literatures', *patter*, 15 June, available: https://patthomson.net/2020/06/15/reading-against-the-literatures-litreview/ [accessed 12 April 2022].

Tidwell, D. and L. Fitzgerald (2004) 'Self-study as teaching' in Loughran, J.J., Hamilton, M.L., LaBoskey, V.K. and Russell, T., eds., *International Handbook of Self-study of Teaching and Teacher Education Practices*, 69–102, Dordrecht: Kluwer Academic Publishers.

Torres, M.N. and Mercado, M. (2004) 'Living the praxis of teacher education through teacher research', *Scholar-Practitioner Quarterly*, 2(2), 59–73 [accessed 6 August 2022].

University of Leeds (2022) *Research data management explained: What is research data?* available: https://library.leeds.ac.uk/info/14062/research_data_management/61/research_data_management_explained [accessed 30 June 2022].

Valutis, S. and Rubin, D. (2016) 'Value conflicts in social work: Categories and correlates', *Journal of Social Work Values & Ethics, Spring 2016*, 13(1), 11–24. [Accessed 6 August 2022].

Weale, S. (2021) 'One in three teachers plan to quit, says National Education Union survey', *The Guardian*, 8 April, available: https://www.theguardian.com/uk-news/2021/apr/08/one-in-three-uk-teachers-plan-to-quit-says-national-education-union-survey [accessed 5 August 2022].

Weber, S.J. (1990) 'The teacher educator's experience: Generativity and duality of commitment', *Curriculum Inquiry*, 20(2), 141–159, available: 10.1080/03626784.1990.11076070

Wenger, E. (1998) *Communities of Practice: Learning, Meaning and Identity*, Cambridge: Cambridge University Press.

Whitehead, J. (1989) 'Creating a living educational theory from questions of the kind, "How do I improve my practice?"', *Cambridge Journal of Education*, 19(1), 137–153, available: 10.1080/0305764890190106

Whitehead, J. (2015) 'The practice of helping students to find their first person voice in creating living-theories for education' in Bradbury H., ed., *The SAGE Handbook of Action Research*, 3rd ed., London: Sage, 247–255.

Whitehead, J. (2018) *Living Theory Research as a Way of Life, Bath*, UK: Brown Dog Books.

Whitehead, J. (2019) 'The underlying importance of content and voice in action research' in Mertler, C.A., ed., *The Wiley Handbook of Action Research in Education*, Newark: John Wiley and Sons.

Whitehead, J. (2021) 'Teachers as educational professionals contributing their living-educational-theories to the creation of the future', presented at *SY.N.THE.SI. The Heuristic Teachers' Society 2021 Conference*, 11 September 2021.

Whitehead, J. (2022) 'Critical Reflection in Educational Practice', *NEARIMeet Online*, [video], available: http://www.eari.ie/2022/04/22/notes-from-nearimeet-2-april-2022/, [accessed 5 August 2022].

Whitehead, J. (n.d.) *How Do I Improve What I Am Doing? Action-Reflection Planner for Improving Learning and Generating a Living-Educational-Theory*, available: https://www.actionresearch.net/writings/jack/arlivingtheoryplanner.pdf., [accessed 7 August 2022].

Whitehead, J. and McNiff, J. (2006) *Action Research Living Theory*. London: SAGE Publications.

Winter, R. (1996) 'Some principles and procedures for the conduct of action research' in Zuber-Skerritt, O., ed., *New Directions in Action Research*, London: Falmer Press.

Wood, L. (2010) 'The transformative potential of living theory educational research', *Educational Journal of Living Theories*, 3(1), 105–118, available: https://ejolts.net/files/journal/3/1/Wood3%281%29.pdf, [accessed 5 August 2022].

Wood, L. (2014) 'Values-based self-reflective action research for promoting gender equality: Some un-expected lessons', *Perspectives in Education*, 32(2), 37–53.

Yoak, S. and Brydon-Miller, M. (2014) 'Ethics and Moral Decision Making', in Coghlan, D. and Brydon-Miller, M., eds., *The SAGE Encyclopedia of Action Research*, London: SAGE Publications.

Young, I.M. (1990) *Inclusion and Democracy*, New York: Oxford University Press.

Zappone, K. (2002) *Achieving Equality in Children's Education*, Dublin: St. Patrick's College.

Zeichner, K. (1999) 'The new scholarship in teacher education', *Educational Researcher*, 28(9), 4–15, available: 10.3102/0013189X028009004

Index

Note: Page numbers in *italics* refer to figures.